HOW TO ANALYZE PEOPLE

DISCOVER HOW TO ANALYZE BODY LANGUAGE AND PERSONALITY THROUGH ULTIMATE MENTAL TRICKS.

Author: John May.

© **Copyright 2020 - All rights reserved.**

The content contained within this book may not be reproduced, duplicated or transmitted without direct written permission from the author or the publisher.
Under no circumstances will any blame or legal responsibility be held against the publisher, or author, for any damages, reparation, or monetary loss due to the information contained within this book. Either directly or indirectly.

Legal Notice:
This book is copyright protected. This book is only for personal use. You cannot amend, distribute, sell, use, quote or paraphrase any part, or the content within this book, without the consent of the author or publisher.

Disclaimer Notice:
Please note the information contained within this document is for educational and entertainment purposes only. All effort has been executed to present accurate, up to date, and reliable, complete information. No warranties of any kind are declared or implied. Readers acknowledge that the author is not engaging in the rendering of legal, financial, medical or professional advice. The content within this book has been derived from various sources. Please consult a licensed professional before attempting any techniques outlined in this book.
By reading this document, the reader agrees that under no circumstances is the author responsible for any losses, direct or indirect, which are incurred as a result of the use of information contained within this document, including, but not limited to, — errors, omissions, or inaccuracies.

Table of Contents

Introduction 1

Chapter 1. Mastering the Art of Analyzing People - Body Language 9

Chapter 2. Essential Tools that Give You an Edge Analyzing Behavior 13

Chapter 3. The Importance of Knowing Yourself 25

Chapter 4. Exercises and Practice for Masterful Analysis of Others and Broadcasting of Yourself.. 35

Chapter 5. How to Interpret Verbal Communication 49

Chapter 6. Common Patterns of Interpreting Behavior 53

Chapter 7. How to Spot a Lie 59

Chapter 8. Nonverbals of the Feet, Legs, Arms. 67

Chapter 9. Some mental tricks to interpret a person, lie etc.....77

Chapter 10. Tips Ready to Use for Reading Facial Expressions 81

Chapter 11. Body Language and Voice Basics Revealed............91

Chapter 12. NLP... 95

Chapter 13. Techniques to use with NLP 107

Chapter 14. Personality Development 117

Chapter 15. Signs of uncertainty to watch out for...................129

Conclusion 135

Introduction

That moment when you look at a person and you feel you can judge if they are in a bad mood or in a good one, or whether they are nice people or mean people or anything about them that you can detect, then you're analyzing them. Generally, this means just taking a look at an individual and finding out things about them without asking them questions or hearing any word from them, even though it doesn't have to be just one look. It is that feeling that you can get when you look at the person and you notice the way they move, look around and even stand. There are features that you will see in that person that influences your opinion and the way you understand them. However, what matters most is that they did not tell you anything you know about them.

It is possible that you will take a hurried glance at an individual and believe that you have known something. And then you tell yourself from your analysis that they are upset, or that they look upset or they are calm and friendly. When you analyze a person, these are the kind of things your instinct will tell you. However, you might arrive at a new conclusion when you start discussing with them or even when you observe them from afar.

If you have not talked with them at all, but you already have some idea about what kind of person they are because of what you've seen, then you're analyzing them and you being right or wrong is of secondary importance.

You might wonder why you should even bother with trying to analyze people. There are a lot of different reasons why you need it because it's a good skill.

At least for a start, it will help you know how you can react when you come close to someone. If you analyze a person and they look friendly, you will be able to meet them up with a smile and a friendly attitude too. If they appear unhappy, you will see it as a better option if you come to meet them with a reason in mind instead of just stopping by to say hello to them. If you detect that a friend looks upset, you will want to do a little probing and asking to know what is going on or went wrong. When you're able to understand the way, they feel just by looking at them for a moment and you can get a brief knowledge of what's on ground. When you learn and understand the skill better, your communication with people will improve totally.

If you have not even the slightest idea of how to analyze people, then you may have trouble with interpreting them or the things that they do. You could incorrectly read meanings into their actions or the facial expressions that they make. You may see their face crumpled and just assume that anger is their default meanwhile they could just be upset at a particular situation. You may see someone who looks unfriendly when the actual truth is that they are being affected by something close to them at that time. When you're able to improve your analysis, your life will become better.

If you learn how to analyze people you will know who will be much receptive of those great new ideas that just popped into your head and also who you can stay away from. It will help you know how you can introduce something to somebody whether it's real or it's just something fun and playful. With time, analyzing people will become your second nature as you keep practicing. When you're able to analyze or read people, the way you treat them will be affected a lot because you can now understand them and craft the message in a way that whatever you're saying will be properly received by then.

This skill of analyzing people can be polished with certain acts.

1. Set up a baseline

Everyone has their own individual habits and the particular manner that they behave. For instance, they may clear their throat, cross their arms, face the floor whenever they talk, stroke their neck, scratch their head, pout, or even squint. At first, we may not even notice that other people are doing these things. Sometimes we may notice them, but we pay only a little attention to them.

This kind of behavior are put out by people for some reason. For some people, it is just mannerism while in some others, it can indicate anger, nervousness, or even deception. When you have a baseline of the behaviors that people consider normal, it will help you.

2. See if there are any deviations

Since you have created a baseline already, you should pay attention to anything inconsistent in those baselines you created and the words that the person speaks and the gestures they make.

For instance: you have observed that one of your top suppliers is always clearing his throat continuously when he is nervous. When he is trying to make some new changes to the business arrangements you both have, he starts doing this. You may wonder if there is something about this you should be worried about.

Because of this sign, you may eventually decide to probe more and delve deeper into the discussion and make more inquiries than you would normally be making.

3. Find out clusters of gestures

People may make single gestures or words and it may not really mean anything. However, you can start taking those gestures into consideration when they are clustered or used in combination.

Let's assume that your supplier not only clears his throat but he also scratches his head sometimes, and to top it all, you find him shuffling his feet at intervals.

At this point, you should be very careful.

4. Compare and contrast

If you notice that someone acts somewhat weird when they are with you, there is no need to make a conclusion about that behavior right away. All you need to do is increase your study of their behavior and try to find out if they repeat the same act when they are with other people. The more you study the way those people interact with others, try to know if their expression changes. Also, try to see if their body language and posture changes too.

5. Try the mirror approach

In the human body, there are some built-in monitors in our brain known as mirror neurons and they reflect the state of mind of those around us. Our body was wired to help us understand body language. This is the reason why a smile from another person turns on the smile muscles on our own faces and a frown from someone can also activate our frown muscles.

If we happen to be with or see a person that we like, our facial muscles relax, the blood flowing to our lips increases and makes them full and then our head tilts to a certain angle. When our partner does not behave in like manner, then we can be reading a strong message from it. It means that they do not like you back or they are upset with you about something that you have done.

6. Find out the strong voice

Usually when at a meeting, the most powerful person present is not on the seat at the head of the table.

Those who are confident have strong voices. When in a group, the person with the most confidence is more likely going to be more powerful than the others. They usually have strong voices, a big posture and a wide smile plastered on their faces.

If you are trying to get a group of people to listen to an idea that you have, you will do better by focusing on the leader of the team.

However, sometimes leaders do not have strong personalities. In real life, they cannot make decisions on their own and they depend on other people to make decisions and they are easily influenced.

When you want to analyze a group so you can pass information, try to find out who the strong voice is.

7. Observe the way people walk

Many times, the people who lack self-confidence exhibit through the way they walk. You'll see them shuffling along, moving without a flowing motion or even keeping their heads down.

People who behave in any of this manner will need extra commendation if you want them to do something for you so that their confidence will be boosted. These are the kind of people that need extra prodding before they can get their amazing ideas out in the open.

If you want to analyze a person and you feel you have tried some methods but it doesn't work for you, then maybe you're doing something wrong.

Chapter 1. Mastering the Art of Analyzing People - Body Language

We have many wishes in life but most times we wish we had the power to see through people and know their intentions towards us. Are there times when you look at a person and immediately think you have them figured just by that one look? Did your guess turn out to be right or wrong? Or did you make some mistakes about some little details of the person's personality?

Whether you successfully predicted this person or not, you just tried to analyze them. There are people who are very adept at this and to them, analyzing people is as simple as drinking juice. Yet there are those who wish to have the skill. After all, if you can analyze people, you'll be able to know certain things and how to approach people. You can tell if your boss is in the right mood to hear you talk about that badly needed raise. If you can analyze people you will know when your parents are in a bad mood and know that it isn't the time for you to let them know how you scratched the car. When you can analyze people, you will use the knowledge to your own benefit.

There are several errors people make when they analyze people. You could be making one of those:

1. Ignoring context

Before you read meaning into actions by somebody, you have to be sure that you're not just forcing meanings into things. If a room is cold or the individual is sitting on a chair without armrests, you will not be doing yourself a favor if you think someone with a crossed arm has another motive. Be sure that anything you think will pass the commonsense test based on the environment you're in. So, consider the environment. Before you count something as a clue ask: "is it normal for someone in this circumstance to behave this way?"

2. Not noticing clusters:

If you're looking at a person and trying to see just one thing that will give you all the information you need, then you're wrong. In life, you can only properly analyze someone by noticing the consistent group of actions that they display like touching the face, sweating, and stuttering. When you notice this combined behavior, then you can start deducing why they behave that way.

3. Not creating your baseline

When someone is always jumpy, you can't deduce anything from it because they are almost always like that. But if they stop moving without being prompted, you can then ask yourself if this is the way they normally behave.

4. Not paying attention to biases

When trying to analyze a person, some things can affect the way you see them. The way you judge them will be affected if you already like or dislike them. If these people have showered you with compliments before or there is something quite similar between you and them or they are attractive, you can find yourself being biased in reading them. And even if you think those things do not really affect you then you're more biased because you won't be able to notice when you are.

Importance of Analyzing

Some people understand on the basis of their gestures, body language, verbal communication, nonverbal communication or the way he walks and dresses up. It comprises of primarily-

Studying yourself

Understanding the nature of the person you are trying to analyze

Scrutinizing his behavior

Focusing on the words of another person

Knowing body language

Getting acquainted with cultural difference

Concentrating on social skills

Forming a general assumption on the nature of a person

Interpretation of verbal communication and pattern

Knowing the reason behind his type of personality

Having an elementary overview of the personality of an individual

Chapter 2. Essential Tools that Give You an Edge Analyzing Behavior

The art of reading people is a crucial and vital skill. It's no wonder security agencies like the FBI and CIA employ specialists to do this. The good news is that you do need to be an FBI profiler before you can read people.

From understanding eye movement and contact to reading body language and emotional intelligence – you are capable of reading people. It is essential to emphasize at this junction that reading people is a skill human are naturally wired with. Every time you interact with people, you are reading them.

With that aside, with practice, you can develop your people reading skills.

Why is it important to know how to read people?

The interaction of various people at a time is essential to the survival of man. The ability to decide when not to interact with others is also vital. Also, the better you can read people, the more you can get from them.

Reading People Naturally

As established above, nature has built the skill to understand people in us all. When interacting with people, you automatically do the following:

- You are evaluating them subconsciously. You access their appearance, body language, and behavior. You try to understand their motives and intentions.

- You are also reading them consciously. In other words, you are evaluating their appearance, motives, and body language. In any interaction, you will probably take into account a couple of things about the person you are talking to.

- You appropriately respond to them based on your assessment. This happens after you have subconsciously evaluated the person.

This is the basic form in which all human interaction takes place.

As an example, let us assume some random guy walks up to you and greets you in a friendly manner. Instantly, your brain assesses his style of dress and evaluates him as well dressed, and nothing about him seems off or suspicious.

You might not think about it consciously, but your subconscious is busy doing the evaluation. After assessing him, you return his greeting with a hello. This was the response of your assessment of him (his body language, voice, appearance, etc.).

This shows that to read people, the conscious thought plays a significant role as well. You may subconsciously be assessing them while consciously drawing conclusions from those assessments.

Another example is that you might be at a party sitting in a corner by yourself. Your eyes are traveling around the length and breadth of the room, consciously evaluating the people and assessing potential threats. Your subconscious continually takes in the information from your conscious and does its own check to ensure you're safe. Those "feelings" you get about certain people or places come from your subconscious assessment.

How to Read People

The idea behind these examples is that we all read people naturally, although some people are better at it than others. You can, however, develop your skill of reading people by learning from books (like this) or in a classroom.

We have examined various ways to read people's body language in the early part of this chapter. This is very important to get better at your job or improve your relationship. However, without any prior lesson or knowledge on body language, you can figure out what someone's body language is saying via instinct.

Let's proceed to the basic tips on reading people:

Understand the Basic Needs of People

In learning how to read people, an understanding of Maslow's Hierarchy of Needs is very important. Although not a perfect model, it does teach a lot of practical concepts in human psychology. How people behave, alongside their motives, is determined by their utmost needs and desires. Maslow explains that these needs come from a ground-up approach (Wikipedia, 2019).

In other words, people will act based on their needs, what they want. This could, however, depend on the circumstance, type of need, level of desperation, and personality type. A hungry person, for instance, might just need to fix a meal in the kitchen or walk up to a restaurant. If they don't have money, they might rob or maim another person to get money to fulfill this need. This is where desperation, circumstance, and personality come to play.

We can group the needs of people in various ways. In general, however, after psychological needs come safety needs. If a person does not feel secure, there will be an outburst of emotions like anxiety and fear, which could drive them to look for security.

After this comes love. People look for affection and relationship security after the first two needs are handled.

Next is esteem needs. In other words, it allows a person to satisfy their ego and give their life meaning. While it is not required for living, it helps make life better.

Human behavior generally revolves around these needs. You can see this evident when people act emotionally. Hence, in reading someone, be sure to determine the need and then respond appropriately.

If you threaten someone's ego, be prepared for a verbal attack, since you have attacked their esteem needs. You have essentially provoked their sense of belonging in the world. They may react mildly or strongly, based on the current emotional state and how much of a threat you are perceived to be.

As another example, someone who perceives that their success at an interview is in jeopardy will likely be very mad at you if you block their car, causing them to be late. This person already ties their safety needs to their success at the interview, therefore anything that stands between them and the job is a threat.

On a final note, bear in mind that motives are what fuel behaviors. Behaviors, on the other hand, are the physical manifestation. Hence, motives trigger behaviors.

Understand Emotional Intelligence

Understanding yourself is crucial to understanding others. To understand yourself, however, you need to develop emotional intelligence. In summary, what is emotional intelligence?

- Self-awareness: the ability to understand your emotions and their impact on your life as a whole.
- Being in touch with your emotions as well as those of others.
- The ability to give the right response to other people's emotions.

You are a rational person with limitations. This is one of the key concepts in developing emotional intelligence. What this means is that your brain evolved from the "ground up." This is also the order in which thoughts appear. Emotions come before higher thought.

Maslow's Hierarchy of Needs revealed this very well. This is why security and physiological needs are at the bottom of the need hierarchy, while self-actualization comes first.

The reason is simple - emotions are essential to keep us alive, help us survive, and reproduce. These examples explain this better:

- Fear will keep us away from dangers and threats, even if it prevents us from accomplishing great things
- Anger will help protect our ego and also fight off threats
- Love will help us reproduce and provide for our family and friends
- Anxiety will prepare us for threats, whether real or imagined.

This is the idea, and this is the way our brain has developed, since reproduction and survival are (were) much more important than thinking rationally.

There are times we find ourselves in highly emotional situations which support the fact that emotions are powerful and come before higher thought. An example is a recent breakup. Without a doubt, for the next couple of days, it will take over your thinking. You will be upset and sad, and probably angry as well.

The problem comes when people do not realize their emotions have taken over yet, and those emotions continue to guide them.

Many people invest in Ponzi schemes, for instance, because they were probably driven by emotion. Things might go well until they realize that it is a bad investment and they lose a lot of money. They then realize how excessively optimistic they were, which drove their investment.

This explains how powerful our emotions are, and how they can determine our behavior. This is why working with people's emotions is the best way to influence them.

This is one secret known to great marketers. Marketers know that people rarely base their purchase decision on rationality, so they strive to manipulate and capitalize on their emotions.

People's emotions influence a lot about them and manifest in their actions and daily decisions. Although, some people can be more emotional compared to others. In reading people, identifying the emotion is critical. For instance, if you can identify that someone is:

- Upset, you might not want to make any requests
- Fearful, you could use that to get them to buy something
- Sad, you could try and comfort them

On a final note, whenever you see someone getting emotional, consider Maslow's Hierarchy of Needs. An upset person will have an emotion from the pyramid of needs and considering this will help you assess the situation well.

Know How to Decode Body Language

Knowing how to read body language is a critical part of reading people. Body language is a broad topic, and hopefully the chapters above have given you an idea of reading body language. In addition, take note of the following:

- If they stand with their chest up, taking a lot of space, with a dominant posture while appearing strong and confident, there is a good chance they are in charge.

- If, while talking, they have their feet pointed away from you, they probably want to leave.

- If it's a woman, consider if she is giving out some signs of attraction as discussed in some chapters above. If yes, she wants to take the interaction further.

- Consider if they are touching themselves excessively. This is in a bid to calm themselves down, as people do this when uncomfortable. It could be the subject of discussion or the person.

- If they are mimicking your body language, you have established rapport.

All in all, consider the overall impression you get from the person. Do you feel they are interested in a conversation, or about to leave? Do they appear to be friendly or a threat? If their behavior or body language shuts you out, they probably do not want to be around.

In considering the body language as well, there is the aspect of reading the person's behavior in context. Is the person's behavior appropriate for the context? Is something about them off? Are they dressed normally?

Another thing about body language as well is that it has to complete the entire picture. In considering their intention, you need to examine what their intention is in relation to the overall body language picture.

It is also important to bear in mind that people could intentionally mislead you with their body language. Someone could cross their arms on purpose or act generally uninterested to mislead you. Someone could be extra nice in a bid to make you feel warmer towards them. Be sure to follow your gut.

Understand How Ego Drives Human Behavior

One of the most powerful driving forces of human thought and action is the ego. Ego is man's need to be respected and relevant in the world around. You see people acting out their ego when you insult them, say something that affects their self-image, or even correct them in public.

Hence, anytime someone's ego is threatened, they will act out to try and defend it. No one likes the feeling of being disrespected.

Whatever a person invests their ego in also has a lot to say about them. Called ego investment, it is important and can make the person mad if the investment is attacked, as this is what they take pride in. Some common ego investments are:

- Standing out as an expert in a field
- Distinguishing oneself for a particular positive trait
- A strong cause, belief, or religion
- Social status in life
- Well-being of a group that reflects the person's value

You can understand a lot about someone based on what and where their ego investment lies. Besides, people with lots of personal insecurities will invest their ego in social status.

You can find a lot of people who associate their ego with a local or international sports team. Hence, they take the loss of their team so personal that a sane person will find it abnormal.

The bottom line here is everyone invests their ego in something, even though some people could have theirs in the wrong thing.

Ego is part of the self-esteem needs of people, and self-esteem needs are above safety and psychological needs. This is why it is a primal instinct in people to defend their ego whenever attacked. An insult is seen as an attack on the ego, and people will do anything to address it.

This is why it is the wrong tactic to insult someone when you're trying to persuade them. If you do, the person will address the insult before giving ears to your persuasion. You also need to be careful of fragile egos. This happens when you insult someone even if it is not your intention.

Be sure to know when people are acting out based on their ego. An idea of this will help you react accordingly. For instance, you can capitalize on their ego in terms of persuasion or negotiations. This is not about insulting them, but rather appealing to their ego investment.

A person excessively invested in a belief will not see any sense in other beliefs, so what you can do is limited. These sorts of people will either have to hit rock bottom before considering another stance or take baby steps.

You can conclude when someone is excessively ego-invested when their opinions and rationale just do not add up when discussing logical evidence with them. You see them overreact and lash out at you over simple matters.

An idea of this will guide you in the act of reading people better.

Understand the Psychology of Belief

The knowledge of this is also essential in learning how to read people. It could be simple and complex at the same time.

It is simple in that what you perceive as your identity and abilities determines your beliefs, as it's hard to have a belief that will make you accept your weakness.

It is also complex in that it is a combination of self-serving thoughts unique to each person. However, you can predict someone's beliefs by examining their values and characteristics. You, however, cannot predict it all.

Changing someone's beliefs is also difficult, though not impossible. It gets harder if the belief has to do with their ego.

Merely considering someone's life will give you an idea of their kind of belief system. This explains why a person that's been an atheist for their entire life will not see sense or believe there is a God somewhere.

The long and short of the story is that the ability to know what people believe in will tell you a lot about them, thus enabling you to read them. Ask probing questions, bring up various subjects of discussion, and you will get a feel for who they are. Their response and stance can give an idea into what they believe in.

The ability to decode someone's belief will let you know who you are dealing with.

Chapter 3. The Importance of Knowing Yourself

Getting to know yourself is about discovering the real you. It is more than just determining your preferences, like your favorite music or the kinds of clothing you like to wear. Knowing yourself involves a much deeper understanding of who you are as a human being. You may seem to know yourself based on what people have to say about you. But this is not a proper understanding of who you are, as it is just opinions from other people based on their limited interactions with you.

Getting to know yourself even better would mean you are understanding what your core values are in life. You will also have to take part in some self-reflection as well as get a better understanding of why you may hate someone. Sometimes the reason behind why we hate someone could be that we see a part of us that we hate in that person.

Your Values

Your values are what you find to be the most important aspects of your life. They are your personal preferences on how you wish to live your life. Unfortunately, most of us don't always know what we want out of life. As a result, we end up living a life not always getting what we would want. This leads us to feel unfulfilled and unable to achieve peace within ourselves when navigating through our daily lives. In order to build a healthy and happy foundation to your life, you should determine your core values. Your values are a list of ideals and requirements that are important to your life.

Figuring out what your values in life are is not as straightforward as you may think. It is possible that some of the values that you may think are important to you aren't, because you may tend to spend more time and effort on other things. An example of this would be if you choose to hang out with your friends instead of maintaining a daily gym routine. This means that you value socializing over your health, even if you may say that health is important to you.

There will be many cases in which you will find inconsistencies between what you value and what you actually do. But this is not a major cause for concern as it can take time for you to understand what your values are in life. An example is a person that has a job that does not suit their values at all. This person prefers the freedom of choice, but they unfortunately work at a desk job that consists mostly of monotonous duties assigned from upper management. This is important to remember when analyzing people, as their choice of work does not necessarily reflect a decision that they made based on their core

values. In order to find your way in life, you should first work on finding out what your values in life are.

A simple way to start this process is to create a list of values that you find important to yourself. If you find yourself lost for inspiration, try looking for examples on the Internet. A simple Internet search will lead you towards countless websites that feature lists of common personal values. Select between five to eight of these values which you will then use to create your list. Rank these words from most important value to least important.

Once you have done so, you should then analyze each value by breaking it down even further into words that best describe the value to you. This will help you understand what a value means to you. Remember, the same value can have different meanings to different people. Once you have developed your list of values, you can then analyze this in order to find out who you are. This will help you in making relevant changes to your situation with the hopes of creating an ideal life.

Look at the People You Hate

There is a lot that you can learn from the people you hate. It is possible to dislike a person who has similar personality traits to yourself, especially those characteristics that you tend to deny. This denial could be a result of a bad past experience which you don't plan on revisiting.

Things that you may dislike in a person you hate could be things that you dislike about yourself. This irrational behavior can lead to an obsessive hatred towards a person who shares similar characteristics as you do. It doesn't necessarily mean that they also share the same values as you do, however.

People that have values that are different to yours will not necessarily cause you to hate them because of these opposing values. Rational behavior implies that even people with conflicting values or situations can still be able to function with one another. This is partly due to these people finding neutral ground in their differences and arguments.

But when this neutral playing field does not exist, then one cannot help but feel negative about the opposing person. A big part of this negativity is the feeling of being unable to solve an issue with that person which would have been solved if it were a neutral situation. Observing those who we have negative feelings for can help us learn a lot about ourselves. The same goes for people who hate us. It may be a possibility that we possess similar traits to the person who hates us, a trait that may be highly frowned upon by that person.

Self-Reflection

Participating in self-reflection requires you to take some time to recap on your most previous behavioral patterns, your emotions, and just about everything else that is going on in your life. This is also a good time to reflect on your goals, which can be compared to your current situation or state of mind. It is advisable to self-reflect consistently on a daily or weekly basis.

The most common forms of self-reflection are to write down your experiences in a journal.

Self-reflection is a big part of analyzing and getting to know yourself. It also, to some degree, forms part of the therapeutic techniques made famous by Sigmund Freud called psychoanalysis. Psychoanalysis allows you to reflect and talk about yourself as much as you can in order to gain further insight into your behavior. This study also goes deeper into the subconscious mind by basing some assumptions on dreams and fantasies.

Know Others

You can learn a few things about a person just by observing them. You can learn much more from interacting and speaking to a person. But this is still not enough to truly get to know other people. Analyzing behavior and motivations behind a person's actions will indeed grant you more insight into someone's personality. But when doing so you should understand a few things about people in general. Their actions are not always determined by some sort of a motivating factor all the time. Sometimes, people just are the way they are.

How to Get to Know Others

Getting to know yourself better involves methods such as self-reflection, determining your values, and more. Some of these techniques can be reversed towards someone else besides you in order to get a better understanding of that person. But only to a short extent, as it is difficult to gather accurate personal information from another person. You will need to interview or interact with people in the hopes that they will give you the answers that you seek. However, people can supply false answers in the hopes of hiding the truth or simply by mistake.

Much of your analysis of others comes from basic assumptions and investigations. Even with these findings, you will notice that you barely hit the surface of determining how other people operate. This is due to the fact that people and their ways of thinking are rather complex, and simple answers and explanations will not suffice. This is why further analysis is needed in order to better understand others. A good way to start your analysis is to first realize why people behave the way they do.

A Thin Line Between Malice and Conceit

We all have, at some time in our lives, felt that someone did not care about us. That person's behavior may have come across as being hurtful. But in most cases, the reason behind this behavior isn't sheer malice, but it may just be that that person was focused more on themselves.

Our thoughts towards people are, for the most part, divided towards three individuals. Ourselves, people that are in some sort of a relationship with us (this could be a spouse, family, or boss), and other people for which we often reserve some form of empathy. A large portion of a person's thoughts is directed towards themselves, with a relatively smaller portion towards relationships, and an incredibly small portion towards empathy.

In other words, the majority of people's thoughts are directed towards their own feelings and towards maintaining relationships with people. Only a fraction of time is spent in empathy. Empathy is the rare instance in which a person places themselves into the perspective of another person whilst realizing that person's emotions and problems.

Seeking empathy from others is, then, a difficult task as people have to see past themselves (their goals, problems, and needs in life) and their relationships (work, family, and socially related situations) in order to prioritize their needs. People, in general, will only reserve a small amount of energy for you. There usually isn't enough time for a person to judge you or be mean and hurtful towards you (with some exceptions, of course).

People Are Forgetful

People, in general, have trouble remembering things. If you take into consideration that people only allocate a small amount of thought towards empathy (the larger amount of thought is generally directed towards themselves and relationships) as discussed earlier, then people are far more forgetful when an issue does not concern them. For example, if you meet someone for the first time and exchange names, it is highly possible that they will not remember your name the next time you run into each other. It is easier for them to recall similarities that you may have with them.

If you do pick up that someone is forgetful in nature towards you, it is not necessarily an act of malice, but rather human nature, as people tend to be forgetful. We can easily assume that a person forgetting our name or forgetting to complete a task that we assigned to them is being disrespectful and negative towards us. But we should try and give that person the benefit of the doubt and not wrongfully analyze their behavior as being negative. He or she could simply not be systematic and organized.

Even an organized person can simply forget something on their schedule. It only takes a split second to unintentionally overlook something. This doesn't mean that this person is not interested in you or that particular task. On the other hand, a person may have a good memory or a reliable system in place. This person may take pride in making sure they remember people or incidents or tasks.

People Are Lonely

Loneliness is common amongst many people. The feeling of being alone can contribute heavily towards a person's behavior. The behavioral patterns of a person within your group of friends isn't necessarily behavior that is in line with that person's core values, especially when that person feels like an outsider of the group.

The feeling of loneliness or being without a partner can possibly cause a person to develop huge personality changes that are uncharacteristic of themselves. You can notice the differences in priority between a single person and someone who is in a relationship. The data that you may have gathered from analyzing someone when they were single may not fully apply now that they are in a full-time relationship.

People Are Emotional

In truth, everyone is emotional. The fact that everyone in a room may be calm about a certain situation does not mean that they are okay with it. An objection to something doesn't always have to be an outburst of anger. Many people try their utmost best to remain calm under stressful situations. This does not necessarily mean that they have fully accepted the terms of that situation.

Not showing your true emotions during a situation can come off as being negative behavior towards someone. This might be during times when you are angry or excited. Holding back your response and not revealing your emotion can cause you to upset another person. This is usually because that person cannot fully analyze your emotions.

You will have similar difficulties when you analyze people who keep their emotions to themselves. This does not mean that they don't feel anything, nor does it mean that they are being deceptive. Instead of criticizing these people, you should try to glean a better understanding of the reasoning behind their decision to not fully disclose their feelings and emotions. This will assist you in getting to know others better.

People Are Self-Absorbed

The definition of self-absorbed goes deeper than you think. It includes an imposing and insecure personality that is linking to a dozen more negative behavioral traits. Not everyone, in general, is like this, but people tend to come off as being self-absorbed most of the time. Most people are just out there trying to live life and, in doing so, end up being too concerned about themselves.

There aren't many people out there that dedicate entirely everything to someone else. This might sound like a truly noble cause but doing this will eventually lead to one's destruction because this act places all of your happiness into the hands of someone else.

Realistically speaking, people come off as being self-absorbed even if they don't intend to be. This could be the opposite of dedicating one's happiness to another person. So independent behavior might just be a better way for a person to seek out happiness.

Chapter 4. Exercises and Practice for Masterful Analysis of Others and Broadcasting of Yourself

In this section, you'll find several basic exercises to practice to enhance your analysis of others and influence over social interaction with deliberate communication. Select one or two you're comfortable with and start there. When you've become comfortable with those, select one or two more, and even add other practices you've found elsewhere and learned by observing others. Learning from others, you admire and then mirroring that behavior is an effective process of adapting a more influential behavior. The key is to practice them regularly and to record your results.

Regulate Your Breath

This is a common breathing technique used in meditation and in the practice of mindfulness. Like most breathing exercises, this is designed to guide the individual into a slower frame of mind that most often includes a slowing and calming of the body, as well. The individual is encouraged to listen to, and focus on, his or her own breath. When the mind wanders, gently guide it back to the breathing exercise.

This exercise can be practiced almost anywhere and at most times, but it does require the individual to block out the rest of the world for a solid 5-10 minutes for maximum benefit. There is no preparation necessary, and while it's nice to practice this exercise in a comfortable and relaxing space, it's possible to implement this in a space that isn't perfect. Doing so will actually only strengthen your resilience to block out distractions and concentrate deliberately for 5-10 minutes.

The primary function of this exercise is to regulate a slow, and steady breathing pattern of 3-count inhales, and 5-count exhales. It's also suggested than when breathing in, you breathe deeply through your nose, and when exhaling, you do so through the mouth as if you're blowing air out from your lips.

By adding this breathing exercise to your repertoire, you'll improve focus and memory and decrease stress chemicals in the body. This exercise also decreases the overall sense of anxiety, lowers heart rate and blood pressure, relieves muscle tension, and improves eyesight.

To practice this exercise:

Get as comfortable and quiet as possible where you can sit undisturbed for 5-10 minutes.

- Sit comfortably and close your eyes.

- Breathe in deeply as you normally would and exhale.

- Hold your breathing for a moment on the exhale.

- Inhale again, but this time, breathe in slowly and steadily for a count of 3 in your head.

- Hold your breath for a count of 3 in your head.

- Exhale, but this time, exhale in a slowly and steadily for a count of 5 in your head.

- Inhale again, slowly and steadily for a 3-count.

- Exhale again, slowly and steadily for a 5-count.

- Continue this pattern of slow and steady inhales and exhales at a 3-count, and 5-count, respectively.

You may opt to continue to hold your breath in between inhaling and exhaling as part of your pattern, but it's not mandatory. Do that which is most comfortable. If the mind begins to wander, gently bring it back to the observation of the breathing process. Your analytical mind should be listening closely to your breathing for any sign of faster or unsteady flow. The analytical mind can also remain focused on the evenness of your counts, trying to maintain the slow and steady flow. After a 5- or 10-minute period, you can slowly open your eyes and readjust to your immediate surroundings. With regular practice of this breathing exercise, you will teach your mind and body that you have the power to bring yourself to this peaceful moment whenever you want. This is a personal micro-vacation you can use any time in your day; it feels good.

Try Reframing

In reframing, you're encouraged to take a situation you feel negatively about and put it in a new light; paint a different picture about it. This can be done anywhere, at any time, and takes only seconds or minutes. It can be done silently in your own mind, or out loud. Reframing out loud has the added benefit of strengthening the story, and the emotion of the story, to the subconscious mind with an additional auditory version of the story.

This exercise works well for individuals who regularly overthink, and form exaggerated and dramatic stories based on one small piece of evidence, often taken out of context. Examples of situations that reframing can work well on might be someone standing you up for a date, someone taking the seat you saved, someone cutting you off in the grocery aisle, a stranger giving you a nasty look, and so on. These situations often put us on the defensive quickly, as we feel we're wrongly judged or mistreated. It's easy to imagine a personal injustice or that the situation was done against you, personally.

In order to reduce this pattern of negative thoughts, and to practice positive thoughts, this exercise forces the individual to look at the situation objectively as if no personal emotion was involved. Through this lens, the individual can often slow the pattern of negative thought and put the situation into a more realistic perspective.

There are no step-by-step instructions for this practice. When you notice a situation, you feel personally offended by, stop. Take a moment to analyze what's really going on from an objective point of view. Ask yourself if you could be seeing some of these details wrong and if something else, which is not a personal attack on you, could actually be going on. Imagine a scenario in your mind, where the same situation plays out, but it has nothing to do with you. For example, the person who stood you up could have had an emergency. The person who took your seat probably didn't realize they did it. The person who cuts you off in the grocery aisle could have been in an important rush to get somewhere. The stranger with the nasty look could have made that face because of a thought of their own, and they just happened to be facing your direction.

Read Others in Public

The next time you're in any line, make a point to take your time reading and observing the body language of others around you; both customers and clerks. Note the correlations you observe, and even make notes on your phone about this while you're in line. Take time about once a month or once a quarter to look back over that which you've recorded to analyze your progress and the spots you still may need more work.

Exercise Written Influence

In-person interactions are a prime way to maximize influence, but this isn't always possible. Many times, we interact with others on the phone, in chat, or on social media. If email and text is the way you communicate for most of the day, try writing a persuasive email at least once per day. Plan what outcome you want to see and then try to implement one or two of these tactics to see if you can get the email recipient to do what you want or agree with you.

Try Listening

Listening can be perhaps the most important persuasion tactic you have in your tool kit. Listening to your prospect will give you most of the information you need for a successful persuasive conversation. By listening and paying careful attention to the words and body language, your prospect is communicating, and by listening carefully to the words they don't say, you'll be able to discern most of what you need.

There is still, however, information beyond that. By listening with deliberate intent, you make the prospect feel respected and understood. In some cases, this feeling is the most important part of the transaction.

By listening actively, you'll be able to ask thoughtful and insightful questions. Asking better questions will give the impression that you're already invested in delivering quality. Not only will the impression you make be appropriate, but you will actually gather crucial information that could influence the success of your interaction.

When listening is your primary technique, your prospects will notice this consciously or subconsciously, and they will want to listen to you and reciprocate that attention.

Listening isn't just hearing words; it requires an overall comprehension of the story being told. In many cases, individuals are not as clear and concise at expressing themselves, as you've become. So, listening to the conversation and finding the key components is up to you. Active listening also means paying attention to the sounds, tones, inflections, timbre, volume, and key used by the speaker. These details are also packed with information, revealing more insight into the speaker. By paying attention, you can determine someone's intentions, what they want you to think their intentions are, and what they expect of you.

If you have the opportunity, ask questions about the pieces that grabbed your curiosity, or that you're not clear about. This isn't just another opportunity to prove that you're a good listener; it's a prime time to ask questions that will draw out more information that you're seeking. This might mean asking your prospect questions that will cause them to express themselves in a certain way. You might be able to derive more insights from additional body language and other communicative behaviors. When you listen, acknowledge what's important to your prospect. See if you can determine the main argument and emotions.

Try Smiling

Your ability to smile is one of the most powerful tools to influence. This is true of influencing yourself or others. We've learned over thousands of years that the smile is a sign of happiness and friendship, so the smile helps to lower our defenses. When individual smiles, dozens of influential processes happen automatically.

For yourself, when you smile, you're releasing neurotransmitters like dopamine, and serotonin into your body, which benefits in a number of ways. The body relaxes automatically when you smile. This relaxation reduces heart rate, blood pressure, general pain, and general stress. A smile is so powerful that it can actually strengthen one's immune system and increase one's endurance as endorphins are released.

For others, a smile from you to them communicates positivity and happiness. For them, this is a subconscious reminder of the happiness of other smiles they've experienced and releases good feelings, cultivating a generally happier mood and disposition. It doesn't take much; even a smile that lasts but a millisecond packs enough power to affect those who see it. Recent studies suggest even exposure within a sixteenth of a millisecond is still powerful enough to have an influence on those who see it. The study exposed individuals to images of other people smiling, where exposure for 1/16th of a millisecond still influenced the group of individuals. Another set of individuals was exposed to images of people who were not smiling. At the end of the study, the participants were invited to all come to out to a venue for a complimentary night of music and free drinks. Those exposed to images of smiling people had more interactions, smiled more themselves, had more fun, and imbibed more drinks than those exposed to images of non-smiling people. Remember that while speaking in anger can be used to rouse feelings of aggression, this is not the influence you're looking for. A forced influence is a short-lived influence.

Try Vulnerability

It used to be so, in business as well as other aspects of life, showing that any sign of vulnerability was not good. To show vulnerability was to show weakness, leaving yourself open to attack and exploitation.

Today, that's not so much the case anymore. To display vulnerability, to a client or anyone, is the starting point for innovation and change. A bit of vulnerability, real or implied, makes the impression that you aren't afraid to face the music and you're accountable for what you say and do.

One way to demonstrate personal vulnerability is to be yourself. Often times, we hide a part of ourselves because we're worried about how it will be interpreted and what others will think. To be your true self puts you in a vulnerable spot. Others see this as bravery, and they subconsciously want to follow your lead and be themselves, too. They may not actually do it, but they at least reminded that they want to live bravely and be their true selves.

Try Empathy and Forgiveness

The ability to understand and related to another's feelings and experiences is yet another technique that can increase your powers of persuasion. If you want to use positive manipulation to drive interaction, it helps to know who you're working with. We like people who are like us, so if a prospect is sharing information with you, be empathetic. Doing so generates a sense of inclusion for your prospect, and that feeling of understanding and acceptance is your ticket to influencing an interaction.

Nod your head. Show concern. Show that you can relate to the stress or the happiness of a situation in the same way the prospect has reacted. All of this helps you to be more relatable to the prospect, which builds excellent rapport. The empathetic person has a much better chance of influencing a person or situation if reliability is already built into the rapport.

One of the key points of the empathetic approach is to capitalize on a perfect sense of timing. Sometimes a nod, a smile, an eyebrow raised, if done at the wrong time, can be distracting and off-putting for your prospect. Laughs and smiles, in particular, are important to get right. A misplaced laugh (or smile) amidst a devastating part of your prospect's story, is not going to build an empathetic rapport. It will build skepticism and distrust.

Practicing empathy means you'll have to put aside any feelings of superiority or pride. Where empathy puts you on the same playing field with your prospect, a sense of superiority will take you off again. You can't just try to cover up your sense of superiority; it's not about making sure the prospect doesn't see your attitude. If this is your frame of mind, you'll likely miss most of the details of communication.

Forgiveness is just as important as an ingredient, necessary for some kinds of conversation and communication. If a history of bad feelings has existed between two people or groups for a long time, forgiveness is sometimes the only act that can initiate a successful and beneficial breakdown of those old feelings.

Forgiveness has roots in the survival of our species. The act of forgiveness has, over thousands of years, helped to protect us. When we forgive someone, the benefit of that act is actually our own. It may feel nice to know about your subject that you forgive them and still accept them, but the relief you feel yourself when you forgive someone is tremendous. Letting go mentally and emotionally of the wrongs done to you is cleansing for you.

Forgiveness has also helped us, through the ages, to solidify an effective and efficient social structure within communities and groups. When an individual does something to go against a society's fundamental mores and customs, that individual is often subject to some version of shaming within the community. But forgiving the individual and letting them back into the group once the lesson has been learned is actually a very common way to practice unconditional love for group members. This practice can also strengthen one's loyalty to a group, for having been brought back into the group even after breaking fundamental social codes.

By practicing forgiveness, you build healthier relationships and improve your own mental health and state. Practicing forgiveness reduces the symptoms of depression and anxiety and improves heart health in the form of lowered blood pressure and heart rate. Knowing that you're strong enough to forgive someone can also generate feelings of accomplishment, capability, confidence, and strength. Self-esteem improves. All of these changes in the mental and emotional state are evident in the interaction, making you a calm and collected individual with the confidence and power to forgive. Your demeanor will echo this.

Try Silence

In many interactions that will cross your path, the best response is no response. The simple practice of staying silent can offer huge influence over an interaction. It can be a tricky practice because we're naturally so uncomfortable with extended silence within an interaction. But what you'll find is that when strategically timed and placed, silence in an interaction can be powerful leverage. The right silence can grab a listener's attention. The right silence can shake down your prospect and get them nervous about not taking your offer. The right silence can convey appreciation, anger, astonishment, confusion, or disapproval. Used at the right time and spot, the art of silence can convey many emotions and engage your prospect more, not less.

It's been said of debate and negotiation, that the individual to speak first is the one who loses. Holding your tongue in order to gather an ounce more information from your prospect gains you more leverage in the interaction. This is an early-taught tactic passed down from sales master to protégé. Business owners are privy to this tactic as well, as a defense against master sales vendors.

If someone makes you an offer, you can refuse. In fact, if it's the first offer, you should refuse. The idea here is to communicate to your prospect that you don't need the deal as badly as they do and that you're not afraid to walk away.

You can test this silent manipulation (in an innocuous and playful way) with one of your friends to see if you can influence them. The next time a friend suggests you get together, try the following and see what they do next:

Friend: Let's meet up for a basketball game this weekend.

You: A game, Hmmm.... (Silence)

Let your silence linger a bit longer than you normally would. Chances are your friend will be prompted to say something to justify the Meetup.

Friend: Yes, we haven't gotten together in a while.

Your silence will be a subconscious cue to your friend that you seem to be considering whether or not it's worth it to meet up. So, the next thing they say will be something to support or justify the idea of coming together. Not only will your friend be subconsciously aware that you might not find value in getting together for coffee, but your friend will also get a cue that you might not find them as valuable a friend. This will increase their nervousness of being rejected, and they'll be influenced by you to emphasize their worth. Obviously, this is an experiment you can test out which is short-lived and not harmful. Don't continue to repeat this over and over, however, or you may just lose your friends.

Similarly, to silence, consider using the whisper technique. Place a whisper strategically into the conversation in order to accentuate the call-to-action. By whispering to your audience or listener, you're creating a sense of secrecy and trust immediately. Not only is it an effective method for building rapport, but it sends a subliminal message about the urgency and discretion.

Chapter 5. How to Interpret Verbal Communication

Learning to listen beyond the surface is a critical part of verbal communication. For you to make a good analysis about a person, you must make sure you overcome bias when you are listening to them as that will affect your mind and the truth.

Pitch

This is simply a quality of the voice of a person that can be used in determining what other people think about them. The general belief is that women always have a higher-pitched voice, while men consistently have lower pitches. Beyond gender differences, though, low-pitched voices have been connected to calmness, reassurance, and a soothing disposition. This is the very reason why hospitals, call centers, and customer service outfits prefer agents with relatively low-pitched voices.

The pitch of our voice can be controlled in four different ways; chest, nose, mouth, and diaphragm. People that speak with their nose will sound whiny and high-pitched; people that speak with their mouths have lower pitches than them. When you notice someone speaking in a higher pitch than they normally do, it can signify agitation, excitement, or panic.

The majority of the people speak from the chest, and this is to ensure they are being heard. But then, it can later become tiring, and the speaker will have no other choice than to speak with a harsh voice. However, the best place to speak from is the diaphragm. The diaphragm is strong, full, and it requires much training before it can be used effectively. It is also the ultimate if you wish to speak in a pitch that communicates calmness and authority.

Speech Patterns

The speech pattern is simply the way people speak; it's basically how fast the speech is, and the pauses being taken around the flow. For instance, being too fast with your speech makes you look rushed and can be interpreted to mean anxiety. What people will think is that you are probably just pouring out anything that comes out of your mind without even giving thorough thinking to what is coming out of your mouth. While trying to analyze people, be aware that most fast talkers are probably nervous. A lot of people are unable to stop speaking rapidly when they are nervous or anxious.

On the other hand, people that talk with slow, measured pauses sound authoritative, calm, and friendly. Their pattern of speaking indicates that they are taking their time to think about what they have to say before they say it. However, it is important to say that this can be complicated at times because if your speech is too slow, it might be indicating that you are distracted or probably tired. Your audience can get bored if they observe that your speech lacks enthusiasm. Understand that slow speech may be in order to gain more room for thoughts. However, excessively slurred speech can be a precursor of boredom.

Fillers and Pronouns

Does the person you are speaking with use a lot of filler words? What is his pronoun usage like? Does he pause a lot and fill up with unnecessary words?

Fillers are words that break up the normal speech flow without adding any specific meaning to the overall message. Examples of fillers include "like," "um," "uh," "err," and the likes. All fillers have been considered bad lately, and generally, the advice is for people to avoid and get rid of them entirely.

For instance, the repetition of "um" by a speaker points to some level of insecurity, or anxiety. Most of the time, people use fillers when they have stored information with certain pointers. In trying to recollect these pointers, fillers are introduced in place of long, awkward pauses.

The way a person uses pronouns can provide another fascinating insight into his current state of mind. Specifically, the way a person employs and utilizes "You," "I," and "we" can provide an instructive discourse. Usually, when "I" is being employed to convey instructions, it is a message of authority. "I" also provides a dominating and intimidating atmosphere in such case scenarios. "I" is an assertive choice of word, especially when the person addressing you is your superior at work or an older family member. It connotes and denotes a powerful wish when it is used to request for one.

On the other hand, "We" is the safer option people use when they need to carry out a task, they find distasteful. "We" could also be used to mitigate the potential impact of the news about to be delivered. It is easier to hide behind "We" when firing someone, for instance. It is always, "We cannot continue to employ you," as opposed to using "I." It can also be a route to escape responsibility for a transgression or unpleasant task. In short, "we" comes in pretty handy when you want to communicate that a situation is out of your hands. However, when "We" does not refer to a single entity or organization, it can be an indicator of "togetherness," especially in unheated situations. Romantic arrangements are a notable example of this.

The use of "You" is particularly complex. It all depends on the context and pitch of the speaker. "You" can be made to sound accusatory under the right situations. A speaker that emphasizes "You" may be trying to pass a message of non-involvement or non-consent. "You," though, can also be made to sound placatory. However, most of the time, "You" is a message of dissociation; people use it frequently in a conversation to make it clear that they are a separate entity from the other party. Learn to notice when "You" is accusatory. Pair its use with other visual clues such as frowns or scowls.

Chapter 6. Common Patterns of Interpreting Behavior

Correspondingly, stretching both legs straight while seated upright indicates the casualness of the person regarding the message or the speaker. As earlier on mentioned, if one sits with all the legs straightened and stretched, then the individual wants to induce relaxation and feel casual. At the end of a class, there are chances that you or one of your classmates stretched their legs while in a seated position to indicate that they are inducing relaxation and feeling casual than they were. While this posture appears like just any other posture, it can be important for an individual that is feeling restless. Using this posture, a restless individual can be helped to induce the much-needed relaxation of the body and mind.

Additionally, standing at the same spot for more than five minutes when speaking may indicate that one is not natural with the speaking. Indeed, standing at the same spot for more than five minutes indicates that one is operating under a fixed schedule and a defined set of expectations such as giving a speech or dictating notes to a class. For instance, a preacher is operating under fewer time constraints and expectations and will speak at random but predictable physical spots compared to a minister reporting on a disease outbreak. For this reason, the unrestricted movement of feet through walking indicates freedom of thought, unlike speaking at the same physical spot.

If one taps their feet on an object, then the person is not actively participating in the conversation. One of the best indicators that one is not listening to an interview is when the individual taps on the floor, desk, or wall. The tapping of feet on an object is an attempt to ease the mind of processing what is being said because it is demanding or disturbing. For instance, at one point, you noticed that one of your classmates taps on the wall or floor when talking about an essay or project because the colleague does not feel as good as others do. This behavior is meant to help the individual process negative feedback safely because continued active listening will make the individual get overwhelmed by emotions.

Furthermore, if one knocks against their knees, then the individual is feeling embarrassed or disinterested in the conversation. Knocking the kneecaps or shaking the legs with knees almost touching indicates uneasiness, inadequacy, and embarrassment. In most instances, this posture is attained when one is seated. Knocking of knees or almost knocking the knees against each other is also a way of expressing extreme anger where one tries to process the negative emotion safely. Either you or your colleagues probably waved their knees to almost touching because you were feeling frightened, intimidated, or upset and wanted to process the emotion safely. Since this posture is mostly done when one is seated, most speakers commonly miss it, but a keen observation of the shoulders may indicate the individual is waving the knees against each other.

Relatedly, if one places one or both of their palms in between their two thighs clamped together, then the individual is feeling embarrassed. Children commonly exhibit this posture, and it is meant to indicate that he or she is feeling cornered or embarrassed. Adults also manifest this posture of clamping one or both palms of the hands between their thighs when feeling embarrassed or scared. Fortunately, this posture can be observed with ease, and the message read accordingly. In some extreme circumstances, this posture communicates that one is feeling erotic or sexual, especially when done by one of the lovers towards the other.

If one walks excitedly across the stage when speaking, then the individual is likely to be excited. As earlier on suggested, moving animatedly across the stage or physical area where the communication is happening may suggest that one is happy and at ease with the message and the audience. Think of how preachers utilize the stage by moving animatedly across the stage. Most storytellers also utilize random and firm movements across the stage to indicate that they are feeling confident and involved in the message and the audience. Most artistes tend to move randomly and excitedly across the stage to show eagerness, happiness, and active participation of what they are delivering to the audience.

On the other hand, if one walks slowly across the stage when speaking, then the person is focusing more on the message content over everything else. When the speaker wants to draw attention to the message over everything else, then he or she will move slowly across the stage to ensure that the audience recalls more the words rather than the body language. For this reason, slowing down during speaking may help the audience lend more criticality to the message rather than the speaker antics. It is the reason why most interviews are conducted while one is seated. Even when given an entire stage, a politician is likely to move least because he or she wants the audience to remember the content of the message as opposed to other aspects of communication. In communication, any unwanted message is known as noise and if a speaker wants the audience to remember the presentation, and then, if the audience remembers the dressing or dancing of the speaker, then this can amount to noise. Noise in communication is thus contextual contrary to the broad assumption that noise in communication is always universal.

There is also the closed posture where one crosses the arms across the chest or crosses the legs away from someone or sits in a hunched forward position as well as showing the backs of the hands and clenching the fists are indicative of a closed posture. The closed posture gives the impression that one is bored, hostile, or detached. In this posture, one is acting cautious and appears ready to defend himself or herself against any accusation or threat. While we insist that certain postures should not be encouraged, it is important to realize that they should be expressed as they help communicate the true status of the individual.

For the confident posture, it helps communicate that one is not feeling anxious, nervous, or stressed. The confident posture is attained by pulling oneself to full height, holding the head high, and keeping the gaze at eye level. Then pull your shoulders back and keep the arms as well as the legs to relax by the sides. The posture is likely to be used by speakers in a formal context such as when making a presentation, during cross-examination, and project presentation. In this posture, one should stand straight and deliver the message.

Then there is the crossing of the legs from the thigh through the knee while seated on a chair, especially on a reclining chair. In this posture, one is communicating that he or she is feeling relaxed and less formal. In most cases, this posture is exhibited when one is at home watching a movie or in the office alone past working hours. If this posture is replicated in a formal context, then it suggests boredom or lack of concentration. If a speaker reads this body language, then he or she should realize that one of the members of the audience is feeling less interested in the message and should activate self-feedback. Self-feedback includes things such as am I speaking fast. Should I give them a break? Should I vary the tone?

For the posture where one crosses the legs from the ankle to the soles of the feet while seated, it communicates that one is trying to focus on an informal context such as at home. For instance, if a wife or a child asks the father about something that he has to think through, then the individual is likely to exhibit this posture. If this posture is replicated in a formal context, then it suggests boredom or lack of concentration. Akin to all aspects of communication, it is imperative that the audience generates feedback for the speaker to take into account and adjust accordingly. While some forms of body language indicate casualness, they are not entirely deliberate, and they are merely stating the true status of the affected individual. What is important is for the speaker to adjust the communication by simplifying it, introducing breaks, varying tone, and being sensitive about how the audience feels.

Chapter 7. How to Spot a Lie

Fact is that only 54% of the lies can be spotted in an accurate manner. Research has also proved that extroverts tell more lies when compared to the introverts and not less than 82% of the lies usually go without being detected.

However, the good news is that people can also improve their abilities for lie detection, maximizing to close to 90% accuracy. The big question here is how to detect that someone is lying. One of the initial steps in this whole process is getting with how someone typically acts, especially when they are speaking.

Basically, this is the process of coming up with known as a baseline. A baseline is essentially how a person acts when they are under non-threatening and just normal conditions. According to the Science of People website, it is basically how a person appears when they are saying the truth. To make it clearer, it might be a bit difficult to tell when a person is not speaking the fact if you are not sure of how they usually act when saying the truth, which, to a wider extent, makes a lot of sense.

However, the techniques that are used to determine if someone is lying can be very confusing. As a matter of fact, these strategies can even be very conflicting. Due to that, it is important to think twice before making an accusation, ensure that you feel more than once about doing it unless it is important to go ahead and find out what happened.

Here are some of the telltale signs that someone is not telling the truth;

The Behavioral Delay or Pause

It begins when you ask someone a question, and you get no reply initially. The person then begins to respond after some delay. There is one big question that should be asked here; how long should the delay extend before it becomes meaningful before it can be regarded as a deceptive sign? It, however, depends on a few factors. You can try this particular exercise on a friend, and ask a question like this, "What were you doing on a day like this six years ago.

After asking that question, you will notice that the person will take an invariable pause before answering the question. This is because it is not a type of question that naturally evokes a fast and immediate answer. Even as the person takes time to think about the question, he might still not be able to give a meaningful response. The next question to ask would be this," Did you rob a cloth shop on this day six years ago?" if they make a pause before giving you the answer you need, then it would be very important to pick the kind of friends you have wisely.

In most cases, there will be no pause, and the person is likely to respond by just saying no and letting the story die.

This is a simple test that tends to drive home the point that the delays should usually be considered out of the church of God. in the context of whether; it is appropriate for the question at hand.

The Verbal or non-verbal disconnect

The human brains have been wired in a manner that causes both the nonverbal and the verbal behaviors to match up in a natural manner. So, each time, there is a disconnect, it is usually regarded as a very important deceptive indicator. A very common verbal or nonverbal disconnect that you should look out for will occur when someone nods affirmatively while giving a "No" answer. It might also occur when a person moves his head from one end to the other when giving a "Yes" answer.

If you were to carry out that mismatch, as an example, to offer a response to a question, then you will realize that you will have to force yourself through the motion that you have. But despite all that, someone who is deceptive will still do it without even giving it a second thought.

There are a number of caveats that have been connected to this type of indicator. First of all, this type of indicator is not applicable in a short phrase or one-word response. Instead, it is only suitable in a narrative response. For instance, consider that a human head might make a quick nodding motion when a person says "No." That is just a simple emphasis and not a disconnect. Second, it is also very important not to forget that a nodding motion does not necessarily mean "Yes' in certain cultures. In such cultures, a side-to-side head motion also does not imply that the person is saying "No."

Hiding the Eyes or The Mouth

Deceptive people will always hide their eyes or mouth when they are not saying the truth. There is a tendency to desire to cover over a given lie, so if the hand of a person moves in front of their mouth while they are making a response to a given question, which becomes significant.

In a similar instance, hiding the eyes can be an inclination to shield a person from the out lash of those they could be lying to. If an individual shield or covers their eyes when they are responding to a question, what they could also be showing, on the level of subconscious, is that they can't bear to see the reaction to the lie they are saying. In most cases, this kind of eye shielding could be done using the hand, or the person could as well decide to close the eyes. Blinking is not in the picture here, but when a person closes their eyes while making a response to a question that doesn't need reflection to answer, which can be considered as a way of hiding the eyes, hence becoming a possible deceptive indicator.

Swallowing or Throat Clearing

If a person loudly swallows saliva or clears the throat before answering a given question, then there is a problem somewhere. However, if any of these actions are performed after they have answered the question, then there is nothing to worry about. But when it happens before answering a question, then there are some things that should be analyzed.

The person could be doing the nonverbal equivalent of the following verbal statements," I swear to God..." This is one of the ways of dressing the lie in the best attires before presenting it. Looking at it from the physiological point of view, the question might have created a type of anxiety spike, which can as well as cause dryness and discomfort in the throat and mouth.

The Hand-to-Face Actions

The other way of determining if someone is saying a lie is to check what they do with their faces or in the head region each time they are asked a question. Usually, this would take the form of licking or biting the lips or even pulling the ears or lips together. The main reason behind this reflects one of the simple science questions that are usually discussed in high school. When you have someone a question, and you notice that it creates a kind of spike in anxiety, what you should remember is that the right response will be damaging. In return, that will activate the autonomic nervous system to get to business and try to dissipate the anxiety, which might appear to drain a lot of blood from the surface of the extremities, ears, and the face. The effects of this could be a sensation of itchiness or cold. Without the person even realizing it, his hands will be drawn to the mentioned areas, and there could be rubbing or wringing of the hands. And just like that, you might have spotted a deceptive indicator.

The Nose Touch

Women usually carry out this special gesture with smaller strokes compared to those of men, as a way of avoiding smudging of their make-ups. One of the most important things to recall is that this kind of action should be read in context and clusters, as the person could have any hay of cold or fever.

According to a group of scientists at the Smell & Taste Treatment and Research Foundation that is based in Chicago, when someone lies, chemicals that are called catecholamine are released and make the tissue that is inside the nose to swell. The scientists applied a special imaging camera that reveals the blood flow in the body and show that deliberate lying can also lead to an increase in the blood pressure. This technology proves that the human nose tends to expand with blood when someone lies, and that is what is referred to as the Pinocchio Effect.

Maximized blood pressure will also inflate the nose and make the nervous nose tingle, leading to a kind of brisk rubbing with the hand to suppress the itching effect.

The swelling cannot be seen with the naked eyes, but it is usually what causes the nose touch gesture. The same phenomenon will also take place when a person is angry, anxious, and upset. American psychiatrist Charles Wolf and neurologist Alan Hirsch carried out a detailed analysis of the testimony of Bill Clinton to the Grand Jury on the affair he had with Monica Lewinsky. They realized that each time he was being honest, he rarely touched his nose. However, when he lied, he offered he appeared to be wearing a frown before he gave the answer and touched his nose once each 4 minutes for a mega total of 26 nose touches. The scientists also said the former US president didn't touch his nose at all when he offered the answers to the questions in a truthful manner.

A deliberate scratching or rubbing action, as opposed to a nose that could just be itching lightly, usually satisfies the itch of someone's nose. Usually, an itch is a repetitive and isolated signal and is out of context or incongruent with the general conversation of the person.

Eye Rub

When a child does not want to see something, the only thing they will do is to cover their eyes. They usually do this with both of their hands. On the other hand, when an adult does not want to see something distasteful to them, they are likely to rub their eyes. The eye is one of the attempts by the brain to block out a doubt, deceit, or any distasteful thing that it sees. It is also done to avoid looking at the face of the person who the lie is being said to. Usually, men would firmly rub their eyes, and they may look away if the myth is a real whopper.

Women are not so likely to use the eye rub gesture. Instead, they will use gentle and small touching emotions just beneath the eyes since they either want to avoid interfering with the makeups they are wearing, or they have been redesigned as girls to stay away from making several gestures. At times, they might also want to avoid the listener's gaze by trying to look away.

One of the commonly used phrases out there is lying through the teeth. It is used to refer to a cluster of gestures portraying fake smile and clenched teeth, accompanied by the famous eye rub. It is a common gesture that is used by movie actors to show some level of dishonesty and by other traditions such as English, who will prefer not to say what they are exactly thinking.

Chapter 8. Nonverbals of the Feet, Legs, Arms.

Eyes and Facial Expression

Profound scowl lines: This outward appearance proposes that someone is despondent or they are somewhere down in idea. The profound scowl lines show up plainly on the face, and they impact an antagonistic look on the individual concerned. Interfacing with such an individual must be one rapidly because they most likely would prefer not to take part in discussion for quite a while. It is important to be attentive of this outward appearance as it will help lessen the odds of moving toward the individual and affront them. If you see someone donning this outward appearance, do not expect the most joyful of discussions with them.

Shaking of the head: This is an indication that someone is unsettled or they do not affirm something specific. On the off chance that you happen to be at a get-together and see someone shaking their head thoroughly and persistently, they likely do not acknowledge something they are being told. Shaking of the head is a certain flame sign of difference, and it can without much of a stretch forestall further associations among individuals. It is additionally conceivable that someone is grieving a misfortune, and this should be possible by shaking the head. Cooperating with this individual must be done in a kind way since they are not in the best of states of mind.

Lips pressed together: This is a typical outward appearance for anyone encountering unpleasant feelings and even displeasure. It is ideal to approach such an individual cautiously because their feelings may implode at any minute. For example, a lady situated independent from anyone else in a get-together with pressed together lips may best be disregarded if you have no clue what to state to her. In any case, on the off chance that you are in the disposition to comfort her, you may very well discover a method for collaborating with her, and it will be dependent upon you to improve her mind-sets and make her grin.

Smacking the lips: This is normally demonstrative of gratefulness or general enjoyment at what is currently happening. Smacking the lips indicates clear affirmation to something decent, and the individual is, as a rule, feeling great. If delectable nourishment is laid on the table at an intuitive gathering, a few people are probably going to smack their lips as they sick anxiously envision the heavenly supper. The equivalent applies when someone sees an excellent woman, they may smack their lips in valuation for her magnificence, and this is a positive outward appearance. When you watch someone in this state, it turns out to be very easy to communicate with them.

Stroking the jaw: This is an undeniable outward appearance that demonstrates an individual is thinking hard. At the point when in a social setting, it will be fitting to be easygoing to such an individual as their outward appearance will show that they are somewhere down in their own musings. Moving toward such an individual gradually and affably will be the most fitting method for opening connections with them and be careful about downplaying the small talk.

Gesturing: You are most likely addressing someone who is feeling great or in concurrence with you on the off chance that they are always gesturing. This is an indication that the message being transferred is worthy, and that they likewise support of your organization since they are transparently conveying everything that needs to be conveyed. A gesture is probably going to be joined by a grin and different types of non-verbal communication that show understanding. It is anything but difficult to collaborate with such an individual since they are straightforwardly responsive and liable to participate in discussion all the more effectively.

Winking: Somebody who is winking at you may attempt to convey that they like you and may be keen on conversing with you. In any case, winking is an assorted outward appearance, and it is conceivable to wink to signify course or essentially catching your eye. At the point when the contrary sex winks at you, it is genuinely clear what their aims are; be that as it may, when a companion of yours winks at you, they may attempt to stand out enough to be noticed or just motioning to you. In any case, it is a significant outward appearance where everyone comprehends and makes it simpler for individuals to communicate with each other.

Held jaw/teeth: someone who grips up their teeth is likely apprehensive, irate or potentially unsettled. Generally, this can be an indication of dissatisfaction a holding the teeth or jaw is only one path for the person to adapt to the issue. This is a significant outward appearance that decides the idea of cooperation that you are going to impart to such an individual. They might not have any desire to talk much deciding on their outward appearance. Thus, it may be important to downplay associations.

Crow's feet: This is a major grin on the face that can, in some cases, nearly remain lasting if an individual is feeling great. It is called crow's feet since it structures running lines over the face that resembles the notorious flying creature's legs. An individual with this outward appearance is bound to be open and feeling great, and it ought to be basic enough for you to interface with them. A glad outward appearance opens the entryway to discussion and upbeat collaborations, and this is dependably a decent character characteristic that self-observers search for in forthcoming companions at parties.

Legs, Arms, Hands, and Fingers

Bolted Ankles: When someone has their lower legs bolted, it is characteristic that they would preferably not be bothered, or they have data they are not willing to share. Much the same as the motion, bolted lower legs connote withdrawal of the individual since he isn't that keen on communicating. It is smarter to constrain your cooperation with such an individual since they are not straightforwardly responsive. If you need to connect with them, in any case, keep it short because the individual would possibly be keen on talking if the issue was of total significance.

Putting the tips of the fingers together: Some individuals for the most part center around contacting only the forefingers, others do this with every one of the hands. In any case, it is an outflow of intensity an insight over the crowd of the individual included. Contacting the fingers together demonstrates some dimension of prevalence, and it may be helpful to initially realize the individual before communicating with them. Someone who shows this non-verbal communication is bound to have a remark, thus tuning in and talking less may be the best connection for this situation. An individual with this character will have a great deal to encourage you as far as social collaborations, and it will empower you to ace the nuts and bolts of social aptitudes.

Fretfulness: General anxiety represents itself with no issue since it is a pointer about how agreeable an individual is. Someone who is always pacing all over unfit to stay in one spot at any given moment is characteristic of an apprehensive or upset individual. Such an individual is probably going to have their feelings running high. Thus, collaboration ought to be limited since it would not be conceivable to decide how fruitful one would be in interfacing. Perusing such signs will empower you to know precisely the kind of individuals to talk with, remembering that anxiety demonstrates that someone is exceptionally sincerely charged.

Inclining the body: This is another significant type of non-verbal communication that shows the preferences of someone. On the off chance that you run over someone who is inclining near another person or a gathering of individuals, this is characteristic of his resemblance for them. They are probably going to be dear companions, and people constantly lean near the type of person they trust the most. In any case, inclining far from individuals would be characteristic of a person in doubt, and on the off chance that you stroll into such a circumstance, you could be strolling into a strained situation. In this way, the way someone positions himself in a get-together says a lot about their very own character.

Holding the head in their hands: When you encounter someone in this situation, their non-verbal communication effectively suggests that they are not happy. Someone who is truly concealing their face in their grasp demonstrates an incredible dimension of distress and would presumably be ideal to comfort the individual or let them be. This is an undeniable non-verbal communication correspondence, and it doesn't leave a lot to the creative mind because the trouble of the individual is self-evident. It would most likely be best not to break jokes with them but rather attempt to grapple with their serious state of mind.

Nail-gnawing: Another indication of anxiety is the point at which someone continually has his fingers up in their mouth. The vast majority of people nibble their nails in an obvious diversion to their very own thoughts yet truly; they consider it more when they are gnawing their nails. This is an exemplary kid language, and it may be savvy to approach such an individual cautiously except if you recognize what is making them anxious. Collaborating with such an individual will include a quieted, delicate discussion, yet it is probably not going to keep going exceptionally long, except if they are happy to share the reason for their inconveniences.

Dynamic: A functioning non-verbal communication shows the enthusiasm of someone to participate in movement and may be a suitable individual to connect with. A functioning individual will move around, address a few people and by and large attempt to outgo in a get-together. Such an individual is probably going to be in great spirits and ought to be anything but difficult to approach as they are in a transparently intelligent moo. It is intriguing to test your social abilities with someone looking like these character attributes since they are transparently open to collaborating with nearly anybody.

Nose scouring: Somebody who is continually scouring their nose most likely knows something you don't or is exceptionally energized. For instance, if you happen to have a discussion with someone who is always showing this non-verbal communication, he is likely amped up for knowing something you don't have the foggiest idea. It may be helpful to connect with him further in discussion to comprehend what he knows, and it is additionally critical to keep it aware. Observing such non-verbal communication articulations comprehends the expectations of an individual, especially in a social setting, and is a noteworthy advance towards acing social abilities.

Arms traversed chest: This is a characteristic of someone who is feeling genuine and would like to limit jokes and participate in a useful discussion. This body stance is a mark appearance for any tyke who at any point made their folks cross and needed to reply to them. By and large, associating with such an individual will include a genuine discussion where your social abilities will be put under a magnifying glass. It is imperative to keep quiet and patient when connecting with such an individual or else you will draw their requital. Understanding the best way to deal with talking with such an individual will be a huge assistance in your mission to ace social abilities.

Scouring the hands: This is a non-verbal communication articulation that shows expectation and energy over something to come. Someone who is always scouring their hands presumably has something fascinating to state since they are straightforwardly demonstrating their expectation. Collaborating with such an individual would intrigue since they would disguise the fundamental parts of their message while in the meantime, talking energetically. Connecting with such an individual would be a decent encounter for acing social abilities since it will include you dissecting the individual and deciding if he is being straightforward or not. This structures a reason for most choices when making new companions.

Squirming: If somebody is continually squirming, almost certainly, they are apprehensive about something and would not talk about it further. It is essential to observe such articulations as it helps in understanding what someone is thinking and subsequently sets the reason for collaboration. A restless individual will be quiet and will likewise talk with a great deal of apprehension, making it hard to get them. Like this, the best methodology is either to leave them alone or if you need to address them, remember that they are anxious.

Head tilted: This is demonstrative of someone exhausted or tragic, and along these lines will warrant an alternate methodology when connecting with them. Someone who is exhausted is in all respects liable to tilt their head and gaze indifferently into the separation most likely somewhere down in idea. They won't talk much and moving toward them probably won't change the circumstance much since they won't look have discussions. A miserable individual additionally tilts their head, and they will likewise not have a lot to state since some distress will devour them right then and there.

Drumming Fingers: Somebody who is showing this non-verbal communication is presumably apprehensive and might want to limit associations. Drumming of the fingers implies that the individual has a great deal at the forefront of their thoughts and except if you are a nearby comrade, they would not uncover this data. If you are out on the town and they are continually drumming their fingers, you should need to get into it somewhat more. Dates can be nerve-wracking now and again and discussing it with the contrary sex may make the light state of mind fundamental for the collaboration.

Chapter 9. Some mental tricks to interpret a person, lie etc.

No-one likes a liar, but we all come across some very good ones along the way. And no doubt, we have all told some of our own whoppers or at least white lies in our time. We might do it to save someone's feelings, or because we're ashamed of what we've done or said. Sometimes, it can be blatantly obvious that someone is lying whilst others get away with murder without being caught.

And who can sincerely say that they appreciate sycophantic behavior in others? When we ask for a friend's opinion, we don't expect them to pay lip service or lie to us. What favor is it doing us if they allow us to go out in a hideous outfit just so that they won't have to tell us the truth and upset us? Ultimately, we are going to be a lot more upset when we see the spectacle we presented on Facebook when we had thought we looked fab.

Lying and deception runs along a spectrum and can range from a white lie to deceiving someone out of their life savings. Even trained investigators struggle with establishing what is true and what is not.

Some people make a living out of it, selling products that do not exist. This becomes even easier when it is done over the telephone and you have no other cues than what you are hearing. For instance, a couple was desperate for a loan and they see an ad online which promises that their loan application will be more or less guaranteed. They call the company and a nice, smooth-talking young man takes their details, including their bank details. They pay a deposit for administration costs, which the nice young man says will not be refundable. He even asks them that they agree to that but reassures them that he is almost positive that they will be approved for the loan. Of course, there is no loan but the couple that are desperate for the loan are even more desperate now having paid a hefty 'deposit'. All it takes to earn a lot of money doing this is an absence of morals and conscience and a lot of desperate trusting people.

It could be as innocuous as, "Yes, this stew is fabulous," when your partner is proud of the dish, she's spent hours making. Even though you might be thinking to yourself, "I hope she never makes this again though, so I had better not be too enthusiastic."

Perhaps, though, you find a receipt for an overnight stay in your partner's pocket. How do you think you would tackle that? Do you think if you addressed the problem that you could spot the tell-tale signs that they might be lying?

How can we tell if someone is lying to us?

Are they touching their noses? Or trying to cover their mouths? They might to hide the fact that they are lying and be nervous about giving anything away so that their hand is drawn to their face to obliterate signs of lying.

Are they looking you straight in the eyes or looking down, unable to meet your eyes. Hopefully, that's because they are feeling shame at being insincere. Sometimes, when people are lying, they look to the left because they are trying to conjure up the image they are projecting and trying to think of credible answers to your questions. If their eyes go to the right, they are trying to remember things that they have heard or seen. Don't confuse a lack of eye contact with a lack of confidence though. Quite often, people who have low self-esteem find it difficult to look someone in the eye. Normally, it's around 50% of the conversation. Conversely, if someone makes a point of looking you straight in the eyes for the whole conversation, it might feel unnatural because it is. It's what's known as the bare-faced lie.

Does the tone of their voice change? Quite often, when people lie a subtle change in tone can be detected. On the other hand, the change could be quite marked to indicate that they perceive an accusation as audacious. Or it may be that the language they use is different too. If a lie is pre-determined they might have thought up elaborate details, which someone who is telling the truth would not so readily divulge at such length. Are they stammering? Or do you notice that they cough to clear their throat, giving them time to think up the next lie?

Does their body go rigid? When someone is relaxed, they tend to be more fluid in their movements, perhaps using their hands for expression. When they are lying, they try and control clues, which might escape to give the game away and so hold themselves tightly in check.

Is there a mismatch between what they are saying and what they are thinking? This might be congratulating someone on a promotion, but their tone of voice is anything but congratulatory. Instead, their face might exhibit contempt because they are thinking that the promotion is undeserved. Don't turn your back on this person!

Are there a lot of pauses between answers or sentences? This could mean that the person is putting a lot of thought into what they are saying or that they are taking their time to thinking up believable stories.

Are they adding a lot of details to their account? Have you ever heard someone say that they made up such a good story that they believed it themselves? This could almost be true. The liar is so convinced that their story is realistic they are also convinced that the person they are telling it to must believe it too.

- Are they becoming defensive and trying to shift the blame? Does their tone rise? Are they blushing? Are they going pale?

This is not an exhaustive list, but the point is that you should combine as many signals together as possible. If a person you know is acting out of character, then it is highly likely that something is amiss. Investigate it further. Ask questions and watch carefully for reactions.

Chapter 10. Tips Ready to Use for Reading Facial Expressions

Is it possible to know the personality of people by simply looking at their faces? Read on for more information. We already know the study of people's face, physiognomy, existed from the times of Aristotle who referred to this science that connects people's faces to their personality traits and characteristics.

While the popularity of physiognomy ebbed and flowed through the history of mankind, its modern version started its run after the American Revolution. A set of pocket guidebooks were published by a Swiss enthusiast. In these books, the author gave easy-to-follow and quick tips on how to read faces while on the move. These books became very popular and it was during this time that George Washington's huge nose became popular as being reflective of his powerful inner personality.

Facial profiling has become very popular today and there are technology companies set up who create software which can profile a person based on his or her facial features. Yes, it may sound a bit weird but there are technologies like this available and used by law enforcement agencies all over the world.

Before we go into the aspect of how these law enforcement agencies use the rather path-breaking technology, let us understand the theory behind facial profiling. The software and hardware needed to do profiling of the face is not simple and consists of many complex layers and experts from various fields including those in facial analysis, computer vision, psychology, machine learning, marketing, and technology come together to create something tangible and useful for society.

So, why is facial profiling technology useful? These elements facilitate our ability to make improved choices about the person sitting in front of you physically or if you are seeing the individual on a computer screen.

Additionally, the face reveals the personality traits of the person. Taking into consideration the huge growth in the use of social media platforms, video cameras, and smartphones, pictures and images are freely available everywhere for facial profiling companies to employ and check out the veracity of the technology they are building.

Reading and analyzing faces accurately are extremely useful elements in making the right decisions about people and improve our own communication with them effectively based on first impressions. Facial profiling technology can affect the working and growth of multiple industries helping in the identification of:

- An effective academic researcher
- A professional poker player
- Extroverts and introverts

- White-collared criminals like pedophiles and others who manage to commit crime and get away

In fact, this kind of facial profiling technologies can be very useful in solving crimes and it is believed that security agencies across the world are keen on working with the companies that develop them.

THE THEORY BEHIND FACIAL PROFILING

Facial profiling technologies are based on the assumption that our face reflects our true personality in the following ways:

- Life science and social science studies have been able to prove that our personalities are affected by our genes

- Our faces reflect what we carry in our DNA

There are multiple research studies conducted by life science experts that reveal our genetic composition makes us who we are more than our external upbringing and other factors that surround us during our growth phase. These studies were done on a number of twins who were asked different kinds of questions such as:

- Are you happy with your achievements in life?

- Do strong opinioned people affect you and your opinions?

By analyzing answers to these kinds of personality-based questions, the research studies were able to reveal our genetic makeup is far more influential on our personality types than our upbringing and social conditioning and other such external factors. It was possible to prove that identical twins sharing the same DNA came up with very similar answers and their personality trait matched far more than non-identical twins. Psychologists also opined that the more powerful the genetic connection the stronger the family traits are carried forward.

Other studies which tried to connect genetic makeup with facial features were also proved to be right. Three of five genes were found to have contributed to how the face of an individual is formed. Therefore, it is quite clear that genes influence the way our faces turn out!

CURRENT USES OF FACIAL MAPPING TECHNOLOGIES

Facial mapping or profiling, as already explained has been happening for a long time now, and thanks to the computing power available today, it has reached new heights. Imagine having access to computing software that can use the features on your face and tell you what kind of a person you are. Recently, there have been instances when a facial profiling technology of an upcoming firm was able to predict 2 of the 3 winners in an international-level poker game.

Facial mapping technologies are also used to find out personality types and traits too. Recruiters can embed the software into their applications. Using images from real-time or video or camera recorders, the software will be able to return a score that reflects the confidence level and suitability of the candidate for the job applied.

Using facial mapping technologies, it is also possible to analyze faces from social media platforms and traffic cameras to arrive at the personality type of the individual concerned. Facial mapping uses the Big 5 Personality Test referred to as OCEAN, an acronym standing for Openness, Contentiousness, Extroversion, Agreeableness, and Neuroticism. These big 5 personality points are identified on your face as follows:

Openness

A person rated high on the element of openness means he or she is a curious and open-minded individual ready to check out new experiences and new knowledge. They are always talking in the following voices:

- I am imaginative
- I love adventure
- I love to try new activities and new realms of learning

Such a person's image will have the following characteristics:

- A facial expression that is neutral
- Such people tend to wear glasses as a symbol of their intellectual outlook
- 'Open' people usually give close-up shots and come closer to the camera lens

- As they are quite innovative and artistic, they deliberately stay away from any kind blur and colorful/natural tones so as to call attention on their picture

- They usually lean towards saturated, sharper, and high-contrasted colors

Conscientiousness

A highly conscientiousness person is described as highly dependable, organized, and efficient. People who get a high 'conscientiousness' score talk in the following voices:

- I am highly self-disciplined

- I come prepared and am very organized

- I prefer having a plan ready rather than being spontaneous

Such a person's image will have the following characteristics:

- Such people's images always sport a smile

- They prefer a smaller face ratio than those rated high on openness. Their faces usually back away from the camera lens

- There is a lot of color and brightness in their images

- They stay away from sharp, high-contrasted, and saturated colors

Extroversion

An individual with a high 'extroversion' rated is described as very outgoing and energetic. They speak mostly in the following voices:

- I bring life to any party
- I love being the center of attraction
- I enjoy starting a conversation with anyone

Such a person's image will have the following characteristics:

- His or her face will be like a beacon of light and there will be a huge smile most of the time
- The person will stay away from the lens of camera preferring a smaller face ratio so that more friends can be added
- There will be plenty of color and brightness too

Agreeableness

A person with a high 'agreeableness' rating is compassionate and friendly aligning with voices like:

- I am quite trusting of people and don't mind giving the benefit of doubt when there is a conflict
- It is easy for me to feel empathy
- I take a lot of effort to make others feel at ease

Such a person's image will have the following characteristics:

- Nearly all the pictures of such people have a hearty, smiling face

- The image will be bright and lively

- Such people like to have a bit blur on the sides of their pictures

Neuroticism

An individual with a high rating in neuroticism is usually quite a stressful being, always worrying a lot. They are nervous a lot of the time and they talk in the following voices:

- I feel so stressed out

- I am moody

- I worry a lot

Such a person's image will have the following characteristics:

- The pictures of these people are quite similar to the people with a high rating of 'openness' with a neutral expression on their face most of the time

- Plenty of negative emotions on display

- They wear glasses so as to appear as an introvert

- They get personal and up-close to the camera lens

- They stay away from blur and colorful or natural tones

- They lean more toward saturated and sharp colors

So, the answer to the question that we started this chapter with is a resounding 'Yes.' A facial profiling technology will be able to discern and clearly articulate the various expressions on the face and create a profile that matches the individual's personality.

Chapter 11. Body Language and Voice Basics Revealed

If your aim is to get the most out of life, then what you really need is 'body language.' The study of body language-the art of non-verbal communication-- is possibly the most amazing and beneficial development in individual psychology today. It adds a whole new dimension to what you can comprehend about people and a whole new set of possibilities as to what you can achieve in the world.

Mind-reading

Body movement not only gives you additional info about other people and about yourself, it also gives you different information While people's words tell you only what they consciously really want you to know, their body language tells you an entire variety of other things, much of which they might not know they're exposing, and even understand themselves. People's fundamental character, the role they're playing the feelings they feel, the direction of their thoughts, their relationships with others-- not to mention what they actually think about you-body language communicates everything. And whereas people's words can hide a wide variety of tricks, their body language is a lot harder to fake.

Similarly, naturally, your own body language will whether you like it or not-transmit information about yourself to others. The bad news is that your nonverbal communication is making declarations about you all the time, and some of these may be things you are attempting to hide. The bright side is that properly and genuinely used, body language can mention what you could not perhaps say out loud, in a way that actually reaches other individuals. I am competent ... I really need your support ...! like you. I love you.'

Body language isn't only about communication, however. What psychologists have realized over the past decennium is that if you change your nonverbal communication, you can actually change all kinds of things about your approach to life. You can, for example, modify your state of mind before going to a party, develop a better feeling towards your partner or feel more confident at work.

Words of warning

Because nonverbal communication is such an effective tool, you need to take care when using it. So, before you begin, a few words of caution!

First, it's a misconception that nonverbal communication allows you to read a person like a book.

Using body language successfully isn't about neglecting the words.

Do not think you can use body language to get others to do what you really want. People aren't fools. If you try using non-verbal techniques so as to manipulate a person into liking you then naturally they will respond to what you do - but they are going to also respond far more highly to those of your actions that expose your control. They'll sign up, typically automatically, your incorrect smile, your moving eyes, your nervous stutter-- and will act accordingly. So, if you're expecting to be able to rule the world through body language, you're going to be disappointed.

Practice makes perfect

How can you best usage body language? The first step is to develop your powers of observation, collecting as much knowledge as possible when you interact with others. Looking is the most apparent way and probably the channel through which you are going to acquire most information. Listen, too, not so much to individuals' real words but to the way those words are said, the way voices sound as people speak. Your other three senses, touch, odor and taste, can also tell you an unexpected amount: the heat and moisture of an associate's handshake can give you important clues regarding how positive he is about the meeting, a good friend's body odor will actually shift if she ends up being frightened throughout a scary film; a lover's taste will change as he ends up being aroused.

As you be more expert, you will be able to see not only the more obvious macro-clues, such as people's gestures or facial expressions. You'll also have the ability to identify the much more subtle and even more fascinating 'micro clues.' So, although in the beginning you might spot only the macro clue of a person's upset clenched fist, in time you are going to also register the micro-clue of their skin color change when they just begin feeling inflamed. With practice, your proficiency of micro-clues will let you understand - and even anticipate - just how those around you are thinking and feeling, and so be one step ahead all the time.

Pay attention to your own body language, too: you yourself are a major source of info, Screen your external signs, noticing how, as you respond to what's happening, your body position changes, your movements adjust your voice changes, your breathing shifts. Monitor, too, the internal signals that only you are actually aware of the butterflies in your stomach that tell you you're excited, the tension headache that notifies you to stress, the internal image of your lover's face when you think of him, the internal noise of a friend's voice when you imagine speaking with her. These are vital signs of what your body is telling you.

Chapter 12. NLP

Neuro Linguistic Programming, or NLP, is the procedure by which the human personality makes a reality dependent on tactile info, sentiments and language that is then placed into perceptible examples. These examples are then utilized by the intuitive to decide how an individual ought to react to circumstances physically and inwardly.

Having a cognizant familiarity with this procedure enables an individual to make their own world. At first this may sound somewhat shocking to the easygoing onlooker, anyway its reason depends on science as we become increasingly acquainted with how the human personality works. At the point when somebody gets oneself in a circumstance that may not be bringing the ideal outcomes, the capacity to change the result in a moment is an incredible asset.

Illustrative frameworks depend on the faculties and how every individual like to acclimatize and process new data. Some want to imagine it, some need to talk about it and others may need to "feel" it. Contingent upon an individual's favored authentic style, managing them in that equivalent style may influence them in your mind. You are imparting a similar idea or thought; however, you are doing it so that sounds good to them.

Very much framed results are actualized by plainly characterizing the ideal results and expressing them in a positive way. As opposed to stating what you don't need, unmistakably state what you do need. When you have your ideal outcomes unmistakably characterized, you'll have to give the thought setting through envisioning the result with the related physical things you may understanding. For instance, you need to imagine the sound of someone's voice, the encompassing commotion you would hope to hear or any scents or different things you may encounter once the objective is accomplished.

Imparting the result to others as such enables them to see the profit and can carry them in your mind. Making your ideal result convincing enough to others will give them the longing to accomplish a similar objective. Numerous publicists utilize this representation to allure clients to purchase their item by portraying what their life would resemble on and when they obtained a specific item. This representation encourages the client to "see" the objective of a glad life.

Displaying greatness is another system utilized under the NLP umbrella. By demonstrating yourself on a fruitful individual, or reflecting another person who has had achievement, you are taking on their conviction framework and their world. You likewise increase extra understanding into why they settle on the choices they do and how their convictions impact the decisions they make. When addressing somebody utilizing their conviction framework, you are bound to persuade them regarding the legitimacy of your contemplations and thoughts.

These strategies can be applied to numerous circumstances and are progressively being used in the business world. How effective do you figure an individual could become in the event that they could legitimately impact the activities of their colleagues? Having the option to impact everyone around you isn't really a type of control yet a cooperative energy of sorts that enables people to push ahead on the whole with one reason. Having everybody in agreement and without singular wants at the top of the priority list implies that the result is bound to be agreeable to everybody

NLP has numerous utilizations in business and one of the key uses is to pick up impact over other individuals. How might you want to have the option to impart in a manner that empowered you to effortlessly communicate as the need should arise to individuals at all various degrees of an association? How might you want to have the option to persuade somebody to accomplish something just by your utilization of explicit language designs? How might you want to have the option to assist individuals with conquering their issues so as to make them progressively effective and profitable. How might you like have the option to impact client decisions by speaking with them at an oblivious level so they simply get a positive sentiment about your item or support and acknowledge your recommendations?

NLP Communication Model

How can it work? All things considered, NLP instructs you that we as a whole have certain inclinations by the way we think, how we speak to the world to ourselves. On and when we can comprehend the manner in which that we figure, at that point we can impact how we think.

For instance. We as a whole have a favored framework for deciphering what goes on in our lives into our musings. We either like to utilize our feeling of sight, sound, or contact. In the event that we have a favored feeling of sight, at that point we will interpret effectively what we experience into pictures in our mind. On and when we have a favored feeling of touch, at that point we will effortlessly make an interpretation of that into interior emotions and so forth.

Let's state that we have an inclination for sight, or pictures. This will get clear in addition to other things in the things that we state, "see you later," "I can see that event," "Out of the picture and therefore irrelevant" and so forth. All expressions that include the feeling of sight.

On and when we have an inclination for contact, at that point we may make statements like "look you up some other time," "you can clutch that idea," "I get a positive sentiment when I think about that" all expressions that include a physical feeling of touch or feeling.

Thus, in the event that we know this, at that point we can tune in to what individuals state, and we can determine what their favored vehicle of correspondence is. We can increase oblivious impact over them by utilizing their favored arrangement of correspondence back to them. Thus, we will utilize words and expressions that they use so as to do this.

Have you seen that individuals like individuals who resemble them? Do you and your companions have normal interests? This is the means by which it works.

Give this a shot next time you are conversing with them. Watch their shoulders go here and there as they breath in and out and duplicate them. In this way, when they breath in, you breath in, when they breath out, you breath out. Notice how it gives you an oblivious association with them. They won't realize what you have done however they will feel progressively associated with them and they will like you all the more subliminally.

One of the significant commitments NLP has made to self-awareness and life improvement is its applications to correspondence both inside and outside. NLP offers numerous functional methods to enable us to participate in increasingly important cooperations with people around us by constraining a significant number of the hindrances to viable correspondence. This article will take a gander at a portion of the manners in which NLP can improve our relational abilities explicitly with others, and in doing so upgrade the nature of our lives.

Called Neuro Linguistic programming for an explanation, NLP is centered around the language designs associated with the manner in which we speak with ourselves as well as other people. Language designs, explicitly the words we use and how we use them profoundly affect our experience of consistently life. At the point when we have an encounter of any sort, at that point we give a mark to that understanding, the name, or the words we use BECOME the experience. For instance, you come back from a day at Disneyland and somebody asks you how it was. You may answer it was wonderful, fabulous, exciting, startling, energizing, fun, heart siphoning or insane... whichever word you decide to depict the experience, IS the experience. Let's assume you picked 'frightening'. Extremely the word 'frightening' is nothing, it's only a mix of letters. And yet startling is a believing, a lot of contemplations and mental symbolism that is related to that blend of letters. Think about this: Imagine on and when you didn't have a clue about the word startling? For reasons unknown it had been overlooked from your jargon, or you'd never heard it said as a kid. OK realize that how will generally be 'terrified'? It's accounted for that some little island countries don't have a word for 'war'... Envision how that influences their lifestyle!

Words cause compound responses in our brains. The things we state or hear said to us, especially the words that they are said in, cause us to feel certain ways about things and respond in specific manners to specific conditions.

How would you answer when somebody asks "How are you?"? Do you carelessly answer "Fine" or "alright". How would you feel when you state that? How would you feel after you have said it?

Imagine a scenario where you answered "Remarkable!", "Extremely Superb", or "Awesome. Do you figure you would feel in an unexpected way? Two individuals can have similar encounters every day, except one can mark them "alright" and one can call them "Great" and as an outcome one individual will FEEL wonderful and one will physically feel OK.

Do you see the intensity of words yet?

If not, consider it in a progressively outside correspondence type setting. Let's assume somebody has recently given you their feeling on something and you answer "I don't know I agree"... Do you figure this would make the individual feel distinctively to on and when you said "You're WRONG". The two answers have demonstrated a similar importance... you don't concur with them, yet the words utilized make significantly various responses thus enormously impact the connection between the two individuals. Alright, OK you get it, words impact how we feel.

As a Life mentor and NLP ace specialist. NLP is a groundbreaking technique that can assist you with getting the outcomes you need in all aspects of your life. By utilizing the accompanying procedure, you will have the option to tweak your objectives, find what you truly need and the means, to accomplish it!

1. Positive

What do you need? This must be expressed in the positive as your subliminal personality doesn't have the foggiest idea about the contrast among constructive and contrary

Did you realize that residence in the negative can really be awful for your wellbeing!

2. Tangible explicit

By what method will you know when you have it?

What will you do when you get it?

What will you see, hear and feel like when you have it?

3. Contextualized

Where and when would you like to have it?

Where and when do you not need it?

4. Self attainable

It is significant that the objective must be inside your very own domain of impact for example is something over which you have control.

What assets do you should have the option to accomplish it?

What do you have to do to accomplish it?

Is this something which you, yourself, can accomplish? Or then again does it necessitate that other individuals carry on with a specific goal in mind?

5. Natural

What are the favorable circumstances and the weaknesses? There are consistently inconveniences in rolling out an improvement - being aware of these keeps you 'at cause' by settling on it your decision.

What are the upsides of rolling out this improvement?

What are the disservices of rolling out this improvement?

What will accomplishing this lose you? Become?

6. Beneficial

This is the inspiration question. Which of your qualities will be satisfied by accomplishing this objective?

What's critical to you about getting it?

What will this objective assist you with abstaining from feeling?

What is the advantage of this objective?

7. The initial step

Do you have an initial step? So as to transform your fantasy into a solid reality you pole venture out, without it you won't gather up adequate speed to make you to the following stride.

Use NLP to Create Changes and Shifts for Others During Ordinary Conversations

Discussing successfully with other individuals is a fundamental ability that couple of are extremely ready to accomplish. Since individuals learn and process data in an unexpected way, your individual style may not concur with the individual you're addressing. This dissimilarity in correspondence styles regularly prompts mistaken assumptions and hard emotions.

Consider the possibility that you had the capacity to quickly set up affinity with anybody. On and when you right now feel cumbersome when meeting new individuals, you are not conveying viably and could be losing commonly compensating connections. The capacity to make an association with somebody finishes you pretty much every part of your life. Personal, business and easygoing connections are altogether affected by your capacity to enough convey in a way that is effectively comprehended and generally welcomed.

NLP offers a few procedures that enable you to express what is on your mind just as to comfort the other party. In the event that they are in a casual perspective, they will be increasingly open to your thoughts and perspectives.

Animals in the normal world do almost no correspondence through vocal language. Just individuals depend exclusively on the expressed word to demonstrate our contemplations, emotions, thoughts and by and large perspective. While watching other living things, it turns out to be very evident that a discussion is going on that we don't hear yet that they unmistakably get it. Not clear to most people, we also have an implicit exchange that we use to convey our perspective to other people. What we know as non-verbal communication is frequently disregarded or not taken note. NLP utilizes this implicit language now and again to build up affinity and a feeling of recognition.

This is accomplished by discreetly watching the non-verbal communication of the other individual. When you get a feeling of their stance, characteristics and manner of speaking, you can start the way toward coordinating and reflecting these practices. There is inquire about that emphatically proposes we like individuals who are most similar to us. By imitating the conduct of another person, you are comforting that person and making the person in question increasingly responsive to loosened up discussion. Along these lines, they will tune in to what you need to state with a receptive outlook and can be emphatically impacted.

Implanted directions are questions that lead with a recommendation of an idea or thought that at that point becomes planted in the audience members mind. An inquiry that starts with "What might it be like..." makes the audience picture their answer before vocalizing it. Giving an idea setting makes it a reality and by posing these sorts of inquiries, you are giving your audience another reality and changing their conviction framework.

In spite of the fact that NLP could be viewed as a training that is utilized for control and control, it ought to be utilized as a positive impact for you and your general surroundings. At the point when utilized in a valuable way, NLP can decidedly change your world and the truth of others that you come into contact with regularly. This positive impact reduces strife and fortifies connections.

Chapter 13. Techniques to use with NLP

No matter what your personal code of ethics is like, you will find that dark NLP can be used in a way that helps to benefit yourself and helps you to reach your goals. Now it is time to take a look at some of the different NLP techniques that you can use in order to help make a major transformation in your own life and to ensure that you are able to get other people to react in the way that you want.

Dissociation

The first thing that we are going to take a look at is a process that is known as dissociation. Have you ever entered into a certain situation and just had a really bad feeling about it right from the start? Or maybe there are certain situations where you are going to start feeling sad or down each time that you experience it. Or you may have some situations at work that are going to make you pretty nervous, such as a situation where you need to speak publicly.

These situations show the whole range of emotions that you can have, and often they are going to seem like things that you have to deal with, ones that are automatic, and unstoppable. But you will find that using the techniques from dark NLP, and using dissociation, you will be able to turn these feelings away and not allow them to bother you any longer. Some of the ways that you can make this happen includes:

1. Identify the emotion that you want to spend some time on, the one that you want to target and get rid of. This can be any kind of emotion that you want such as disliking the situation, discomfort, rage, and fear.

2. Once you have picked out the feeling that you want to work with, you can imagine that you have the ability to float out of your body, and then look back at yourself. This gives you a chance to encounter the whole situation from a different perspective, of that of the observer.

3. Once you take yourself out of the situation and just get to watch what is going on, rather than needing to actively participate in it, you will find that your own personal feelings about that particular situation will start to change.

4. You may find that you don't feel as shy, that the public speaking isn't as big of a deal as you had thought, or maybe you are now able to talk to that person you liked, the one who made you feel nervous in the beginning.

5. To get an added boost to this, you can first imagine that you are able to float out of your body looking at yourself, and then you can float out of this body again so that you can look at yourself looking at yourself. This is a process that is known as double dissociation and it can ensure that you are really removed from the situation and that all of the negative emotions that come with many minor situations are long gone so that you are better able to handle them.

Future Pacing

This is another technique that you can work with where you will ask a person to imagine that they are doing something in the future, and then you will monitor the reaction that they have to this. It is typically something that is going to be used in order to check that a change process has been successful. You can check this out by observing the body language of the target when this person is going through a difficult situation before and also after the intervention.

If you are doing this and notice that the body language is the same, then you know right away that the intervention has not been successful the way that you would like.

This method is going to be based on the ideas and methods that come with visualization, where the mind is going to be assumed to not have the ability to tell the difference between when a situation is real, and one that has been visualized in a clear manner.

The theory of this is that, once the person has taken the time to visualize the experience in a positive way, when they do actually encounter the situation, the visualized situation that they did before is going to be their model for how to behave in that situation, even those they only imagined and made up the visualization. The mind is not really able to come up with the differences between the real-life scenario and the imagined one, which can help the person to get through that whole situation much easier.

So, how is this going to be useful for the person who is trying to work with dark NLP? If you are worried about a specific situation, then the idea of future pacing is going to be able to help you out here. Before entering into that situation, take some time to visualize it in your head. Think about it in a positive way, imagining what it will feel like if that situation goes really well, above your own expectations, and if you were able to get through it without a hitch?

Try to imagine this as clearly as possible. Let's say that you are anxious about a job interview. Imagine what you are going to wear to the interview, what time you will show up, what you will say about your resume and the answers that you are going to give to the questions that you are asked. Imagine that you are shaking the hand of the person interviewing you and that you feel really good about the whole situation like you are sure that they will offer you the job because they were dazzled by your credentials and all of the things that you said during the interview.

You will find that if you were able to come up with a strong enough and clear enough picture and visualization of the event, that when you actually head to the real event, it won't seem so scary. Your brain will assume that it has already gone through all of this, and the situation is going to pan out much better than you would imagine.

Content reframing

The next thing that we need to take a look at is content reframing. This is another technique that you can use any time that you feel that the situation that is around you seems to be helpless or negative. When you take the time to reframe things, it is going to take away any of the negative out of the situation that you see, and it will empower you by changing the meaning of the experience into something that is going to feel and appear to be more positive to you.

A good example of this is to say that you were in a long relationship and then it ends. You may not have been the one to end it, and maybe the other person blindsided you with the news. When you take a look at this breakup on the surface, it is going to seem awful and all that you will want to do is go and sulk in all of the misery that you feel. But maybe the one thing that you need to focus on here is how to reframe the situation.

For example, what are some of the benefits that you could enjoy now that you are single? You could look at it as the ability to be open to a new, and hopefully better, relationship. You now have the ability to go and do what you want, when you want it, without having to worry about how it will affect the other person or what they are going to think about this newfound freedom. And after that relationship is over, you are able to take some of the valuable lessons that you learned from it along the way and use it to make sure that you have better and stronger relationships in the future.

There are a lot of ways that you are able to go through and reframe the situations around you. There are always going to be situations that are a bit negative, ones that don't seem to work the way that you want, and ones that will drag you down and make it seem hard to get the results that you want. But by simply looking at the positives of that situation, and there are always some things that are positive, and ignoring the negatives that can come with it, you can really start to see that the situation is not that bad.

In some situations, you will start to panic, or even focus on the fear that shows up. And this is pretty natural. But if you don't move the mind away from this panic and fear, it is just going to lead you to a lot more problems down the line, more things that you need to deal with. In contrast, when you shift your focus, using some of the ideas that we were talking about above, you will be able to clear out your head, and really think about whether the situation was as bad as you had first thought.

Anchoring yourself

The next method that we are going to explore is going to be that of anchoring. We spent a little bit of time talking about anchoring in this guidebook but didn't get a chance to go too much in depth about how it works, why you would use it and more. Now it is our chance to see some of the great things that you can do with the method of anchoring, and why it is one of the best methods to help you form a good connection with the other person.

The idea of anchoring is going to find its origins with Russian scientist Ivan Pavlov. Pavlov is well known for some of his experiments with dogs by ringing a bell repeatedly while those dogs were eating. After he repeated the ringing of the bell, Pavlov them found that simply by ringing the bell, even if he didn't bring out the food at that time, he was able to get the dogs to salivate. This was all just from hearing the bell.

The reason for this is that Pavlov had been able to create a big connection in the brain between the bell, and the behavior that would necessitate the salivating, namely, the eating of food. Then, when the dogs did hear the bell again, they assumed that food was on the way, or at least their brains did, and so the salivating started to prepare them for eating, even though there wasn't any food coming their way.

The neat thing about all of this is that you are able to use this same idea in order to stimulate a response that is anchored back to you. Instead of having the noise or the touch or other signal go back to food or something else, you are able to use it in a way that anchors your target right back to you.

Anchoring yourself is going to make sure that you associate the desired positive emotional response to a specific sensation or phrase that you choose. If you are able to choose the right kind of thought or emotion that is positive, and you are able to deliberately go through and connect it to a simple thought or gesture, you can then make sure that this anchor is triggered when you are feeling low. Then, you can do this gesture in order to help change around the feelings that you are dealing with.

1. The first thing to consider is what you would like to feel. You can pretty much anchor any kind of emotion that you would like, but most people are going to go with a good feeling like calmness, happiness, and confidence.

2. Decide where you want the anchor place to be on your body. You can pick almost anywhere but many times people like to squeeze on a fingernail, touch their knuckles, pull on the earlobe or even just touch their wrist. It is important to add some kind of physical touch to this because it allows you to trigger that positive feeling no matter when or where. The placement doesn't matter. But you want to make sure that it is unique enough that you aren't as likely to touch it randomly at any other point.

3. Think about a time in the past when you felt that state that you want to feel now. So, if you want to have more confidence, think back to a time in your life when you felt you had a good deal of confidence.

4. Mentally go back to that time and float into your body. Look through your eyes of that moment and relive the memory as much as you can. You can work to adjust your own body language so that it works with the memory. See what you saw, hear what you heard, and try to feel the feelings as much as you can and so on. This can help you to feel more in that state than ever before.

5. As you go back and relive some of that memory more and more, try to touch, pull, or squeeze the part of the body that you choose. You will feel that feeling swell as you go through and relive the memory. You can release the touch that the emotional state starts to reach its peak, and when it starts to wear off.

6. Doing this may seem a little silly when you first get started, but the point of doing this is to create a neurological stimulus response that is going to be able to trigger the emotion or the state at any time that you would like. If you have done this in the proper manner, you will be able to touch yourself and use the same pressure again in the future, and that emotion and that state will come back to you.

Chapter 14. Personality Development

All individuals possess certain traits of personality which set us apart from the rest of the world. The mix of good and bad traits tells us how you respond to the situation. According to some studies, it is stated that these traits are genetic and remain fixed throughout life.

Lastly, the third factor called character which is inclusive of emotional, cognitive, and behavioral patterns which are learned through experience determines how a person can think, behave, and feel throughout his life.

Other than this, the character also depends upon our moral values which are inherited in us through our ancestors.

The different stages of life significantly influence personality development, which is a very essential part for the person and the other human beings also. Let's discuss the stages of life: -

Infancy- The first two years of the child are very crucial in which he/she learns basic trust and mistrust. If he/she is well-nurtured and loved by the parents properly, then the infant develops trust, security, and basic optimism. If it is opposite, then the result will be mistrust.

Toddlerhood- It occurs after the first stage starts from three to four years. During this stage, they learn shame and autonomy

Preschool- In this, the child learns initiative and shame. Through active play, they start using imagination, try to cooperate with others, etc. During this stage, the parents play a very essential role in which they get a restriction on the play and use their imagination.

School-age- In this stage, the whole development of the child takes place in which he/she learns various good habits like teamwork, how to work with rules and regulations, cooperation, and basic intellectual skills. Moreover, self-discipline surges every year with the passing of school age.

If the past stages of the child are excellent, then they learn various good habits otherwise, they feel inferior in front of others.

Adolescence- It is the age between 13 to 14 years in which a child starts behaving like a mature person. The young person starts experimenting new things and if parents are opposed to it, negativity arises. Indeed, this stage starts seeking leadership and rapidly develops a set of ideals for them to live by.

Importance of Personality Development

In order to get success in both personal and professional life, a great overall personality is very crucial in the life of an individual. Every person is automatically influenced by attractive and renowned personality. Whether it is a job, interview, while interacting with other human beings, and many more sectors, you must have certain traits and features which should compel other human beings to say yes! What a great personality!

Nowadays, in every field, the personality of a person matters a lot. For instance- in the interview to impress the interviewer, in business to influence the client and make them believe in you.

Therefore, the demand of personality has surged drastically with the passage of time. These days with the advent of personality, every school is careful about it and they make their students a perfect example where they can excel in every field.

Some years ago, the overall concept of personality was very common and no one really approached towards it. Parents also rarely gave importance to it. It was just looking good while wearing good clothes, which is more emphasized in a work-related environment. Indeed, the interviewer just wanted good working skills of the person and not interpersonal skills.

But now the scenario has changed a lot in this age of competition and economic revolution. Let's put some light on the various points of personality which are considered very crucial in personality development: -

Personality development inculcates numerous good qualities

Good qualities can be in any form like punctuality, flexibility, friendly nature, curious about things, patience, eager to help others, etc. However, if you have a good personality, you will never ever hesitate to share any kind of information with others which benefit them.

According to the rules, you will follow everything like reaching on time at the office. All these personality traits not only benefit you but also to the organization directly or indirectly.

Gives confidence

Great personality tends to boost your overall confidence. If you know that you are properly groomed and attired, it makes you more anxious towards interacting with people. Other than this- in any of the situation, if you know how to behave, what to say, how to show yourself, then automatically your confidence is on the peak.

Overall, a confident person is liked and praised by everyone both in personal and professional life.

Reduces stress and conflicts

A good personality with a smile on his face encourages human beings to tackle any hurdle of life. Trust me, flashing a smile on the face will melt half of the problems side by side, evaporating stress and conflicts.

Moreover, with a trillion million smiles on your face, there is no point in cribbing over minor issues and problems which come in the way of success.

Develops a positive attitude

A positive attitude is that aspect of life which is must to face any hard situation and one to one progress in life. An individual who thinks positive always looks on the brighter side of life and move towards the developmental path. He/she rather than criticizing or cribbing the problem always tries to find out the best possible solution with a positive attitude.

So always remember, if any problem occurs, then take a deep breath-in, stay cool keeping in mind the positivity anyhow. This is because developing a positive attitude in hopeless situations is also part of personality development.

Improves communication skills

Nowadays, a lot of emphases is given on communication skills as a part of personality development. A good communicator always lives an excellent personal and professional life. Indeed, after your outer personality, the first impression tends to fall on another person is what you say and how you say it.

Verbal communication of the person makes a high impact on another person. Individuals with good communication skills ought to master the art of expressing thoughts and feelings in the most desired way.

Helps you to be credible

It is a good saying that you cannot judge a book by its cover which also applies to a person. Means people judge a person from their clothing and how it is worn. Therefore, dressing plays a very essential role in the personality of an individual.

So, be careful while picking up clothes for yourself. It doesn't mean you will buy expensive clothes, but they should be perfect and suit your personality.

How to develop a personality

I just want to ask one question from you guys that have you observed any person who is the center of attraction? They have mind-blowing qualities due to which people get attracted to them like a magnet. So, how do they manage to do this?

Actually, they are personified persons who want to learn something or everything to look unique.

Well, every individual has his own qualities and traits which make them unique. But, some of the tips are very beneficial which help the person to be a perfect example of personality. While making your personality there is no room of age, but the improvement has. It cannot happen in a day, it takes overtime.

So, there are multiple characteristics on which an individual has to work on while developing his personality. Here you will know some tips on developing personality: -

Be a good listener

If a person has good listening skills, they can make another person feel important in front of them, so be a good listener. One of the examples of this is:

This quality is very appealing in order to have an awesome personality.

Take interest in reading and expanding your horizons

The more you gain knowledge about various aspects, the more you become famous in your personal and professional life. So, read more and cultivate those interests in yourself which make you stand in front of others with confidence.

On the other hand, when you meet people, you have the opportunity to share things with the individuals by making them flat.

Dress up well

While going to the office, party, or on any other occasion, wear dress according to that which suits you. Good looks no doubt add to your personality but what matters is how you dressed up for any occasion. Thus, dressing sense plays a very crucial role in personality development and building confidence.

Observe the body language

While interacting with people, try to use positive gestures which make another person comfortable and relaxed. Some studies stated that 75% of the work is done by verbal communication in which a person's personality is judged by another person.

So, keep an eye on body language.

Remain happy and light-hearted

Try to see the joy in the world and every work that you do. Spend precious and laughing with others so that you feel happy. Always appreciate people in one way or the other. So, smiling and laughing plays a significant role in making your personality awesome.

Stay calm in tensions

Some people have good personality until and unless they come across some tense situation. Don't be that kind of person who becomes angry in tensed issues and shouts on everybody. Therefore, be relaxed and stay cool while finding out the best possible solution for a problem.

Develop leadership qualities

It is believed that good leaders have an excellent personality which can impress another person easily and effectively. However, leadership skills don't mean giving orders to subordinates. Rather, it means how well you can as a leader manage your subordinates to accomplish any task. Indeed, work hard to set an example for them who work with you so that if in the future they will get a chance to work with you, they will feel very excited.

Work on your inner beauty

Most of the people only work on external appearance, but when you behave or speak outside, everything gets reflected. So, it is true that the outer look is essential but inner beauty is also very crucial to be a full-proof personality.

Indeed, it takes only a few days to change your outer appearance but, sometimes it takes years to change the inner world. So, work on that and you yourself can see the difference.

Learn from your mistakes

As a human, mistakes are part of life which makes an actual individual. If you are learning any new thing, you are bound to make mistakes. Always get ready to learn from your mistakes while saying or feeling sorry. Saying sorry will make a significant place to make a respectful corner among your friends or colleagues.

Indeed, if you have made a mistake, forgive yourself and move on.

Always make compliments to others

If you see that someone is looking great or gorgeous, then don't hesitate to say something positive to them. This will make your image or standard up.

Be original

The next essential step in making your personality awesome shows what you actually are. It is a very eminent saying that original is worth than copied things. So, follow this and be how it is; rather, pretending what you are not.

Other than this, one should not copy someone's personality. But you can adopt some habits of other individuals who are good and help you in developing your personality.

Meet new people with a smile

Try to meet new people which will make you aware of a new environment and culture by which you as an individual can learn new things. Moreover, it also broadens your horizons.

Make your own opinion

The opinion is something which cannot be changed or stolen from another person. For example, while sitting in a group when someone asks your opinion, give them your opinion which is unique and is for the betterment of everyone. This attitude will make you more interested and stimulating to be sociable.

Get out of your comfort zone

Be ready and always get prepared to challenge yourself to learn new skills. Like for most people- learning new things is quite a challenging work. But with a positive attitude and confidence in yourself, you can tackle anything.

Don't give up at any point

Whenever you try to do anything and you fail, then give yourself a second chance to improve it. So, don't give up at any cost and try, try, try until you succeed.

Create your own style

According to my personal experience, you don't need to be a replica of anyone- you need to be yourself.

So, find the best style which makes you comfortable and relaxed. This pattern of developing your personality is very unique which offers the chance to explore and develop over time. Means if you get tired of something, you can move to another style without any downturn.

Be passionate about your work

In case you are not happy with your job or work, then don't complain regards to that if you don't have the capability to change the circumstances.

Therefore, figure out your passion and try to make the necessary changes in your life to change the present situation.

Don't make yourself aggressive

Well, in everyday situation there are numerous assertive situations which make you angry. But, be careful because is a big turn off to people, both in social and professional life.

If your nature is like pushy, then be honest to yourself and try to change it as soon as possible.

Don't strive hard for perfection

Keep in mind that you don't have to attain perfection in any field because no one is perfect in this world. When a person is willing to show imperfection, then he/she is putting people at ease.

Evaluate yourself

Evaluation is the best technique to change yourself towards positivity so keep evaluating yourself at regular intervals of time. In this case, take the feedback from your friends, colleagues, and other near and dear ones seriously, which will help you to improve gradually.

Chapter 15. Signs of uncertainty to watch out for

In the event that you wonder on the off chance that you are with somebody unreliable, or in the event that you ask whether you are uncertain yourself, these are the indications of instability that can't be covered up.

#1 They stress over everything. Did I say everything? I mean the world. There is definitely not a solitary thing that somebody who is unreliable doesn't stress over. They stress over their subsequent stage since they aren't sure they will arrive on safe ground. They consistently feel like the subsequent stage is sand trap.

#2 They never have a sense of security or settled. An uncertain individual never feels like they are protected or settled in their own life or in their very own skin. Normally encounters in their past sustain the frailty. They live in a condition of impermanent and they never get settled in light of the fact that it could all be no more.

#3 They pose similar inquiries again and again, as though they can't acknowledge the appropriate response. Like a youngster, they ask you similar inquiries again and again and over. How you answer matters not, they won't acknowledge your answer except if it is negative. They absolutely never put stock in anybody since they anticipate the most exceedingly awful.

#4 They push you away and afterward pull you back in. Somebody who is shaky needs to pull you in. At that point when you get excessively close, they monstrosity out and push you away. Their very own dread of dismissal drives them to continually push the very individuals they need close, far away. At that point once you leave, they implore you back.

#5 They continually inquire as to whether you are distraught or what they have done. Weakness prompts them always inquiring as to whether they have planned something for make you distraught. Stressed that they will lose you in the event that they don't do what you need and how you need it, their stressed nature has no base.

#6 They reliably apologize regardless of whether there's no expression of remorse essential. Never certain about themselves or how they run over, somebody shaky consistently feels as though they have accomplished something incorrectly and aren't above saying 'sorry' regardless of whether they haven't done anything by any stretch of the imagination.

Just so nobody is irate or angry with them, they simply express sorry to learn anything they could've done.

#7 They tend to disrupt their connections. Individuals who are uncertain never feel commendable enough to be seeing someone, causes a consistent uneasiness and dread that they will be discovered and left behind.

That prompts overcompensations to things and pushing individuals away when they dread that things are going gravely to ensure themselves. That can get them the very outcome they endeavor to evade in a relationship.

#8 They feel like everybody despises them. Perhaps the greatest indication of instability is that uncertain individuals always feel like everybody despises them. They can't generally disclose to you why or put their finger on what the issue is. They simply feel like everybody detests them.

#9 They stress in the event that somebody is speaking seriously about them constantly. Shaky individuals stress continually that individuals talk over them despite their good faith. Not having any desire to be disdained by individuals throughout their life, their instability drives them to persistently scan for affirmation that individuals don't care for them and are castigating them. For the most part, when there is no premise.

#10 They leave each circumstance thinking about whether they irritated anybody or aggravated somebody. Individuals who are unreliable are tension baffled practically constantly. They stress on the off chance that they said something rotten and replay the occasions of each snapshot of their social communications with individuals.

#11 They don't feel great in a gathering, so they for the most part have one individual they stick to. Uncertain individuals seem like outgoing people since they as a rule shroud the instability and turn on the appeal.

However, they ordinarily prefer to have one individual to stick to that makes them progressively secure and genuine. Typically, just having the option to have each dear companion in turn, their kinship is their wellbeing zone when out with others.

#12 They strike hard when harmed. Uncertain individuals are continually injured. Their emotions are routinely harmed, which leads them to strike out against somebody who damages them. For the beneficiary, it appears to be an all-out eruption.

Yet, because of the measure of strife and dread going on in the uncertain individual's psyche, it resembles repetitive sound never stops. Only one more thing in a flash sets them over the edge.

#13 They attempt to dazzle you, yet feel like a fraud inside, which makes them an apprehensive wreck. Most uncertain individuals don't appear to be shaky until you become more acquainted with them. Truly adept at veiling the individual so frightful inside, they build up a hard-external shell, which makes them feel like a fraud constantly.

#14 Being distant from everyone else is their most exceedingly terrible dread. For unreliable individuals, being without anyone else is about the most noticeably terrible thing they can envision. They need other individuals to make themselves feel like everything is ok and safe. On the off chance that they lose somebody near them, it is overpowering, particularly somebody they love.

#15 They ache for endorsement yet won't acknowledge it at any rate. Somebody uncertain pines for acknowledgment and endorsement. In any event, when given to them, they don't accept or acknowledge it. Regardless of whether the very thing they want gazes them in the face, they will not see it.

#16 They characterize themselves by what other individuals consider them. Uncertain individuals let other individuals disclose to them who and what they are on the grounds that they aren't very certain for themselves what they are made of. Always hoping to satisfy others and increase their acknowledgment, on the off chance that somebody doesn't care for them, it endures a colossal shot to their confidence.

#17 When you are with them you nearly feel the stirring of tension. Unreliable individuals are only difficult to be near. You can't put your finger on it, however they once in a while sit, they infrequently quit talking, or they simply have an anxious nervousness that tails them any place they go.

#18 They tend to be a fussbudget. Unreliable individuals don't have confidence in themselves, so they return and re-try everything around multiple times. Despite everything it won't ever be correct.

#19 They are envious of your associations with other individuals. Unreliable individuals are very tenacious. When they make you their stone, they get extremely desirous when you connect with another person.

They need you next to them to feel like nothing is wrong with the world and secure. In the event that you aren't bolstering their spirit, it feels vacant. They need 100% of you.

#20 They go overboard to apparently basic things. Since they continually convey a rucksack of apprehension, the littlest thing appears to set them off for reasons unknown. Persistent uneasiness is a troublesome thing to live with and can have somebody hitting the verge out of the blue and now and again making a mountain out of a molehill.

Conclusion

There's much to gain from being able to read others, but make sure you use this ability responsibly. It's very easy to hurt others, so make sure you're doing your best to be a good influence, not merely an active one. The understanding that you have gained about human psychology is very powerful knowledge, and I encourage everybody to exercise caution as they try to implement what they have learned.

Still, the majority of this journey will be a personal one. The more that you understand about yourself, the more you will be able to understand others. Invest in your relationship with yourself, respect yourself, and take care to listen to yourself. You will show yourself what it means to be human. We all work from this position, and we're all more similar than we are different. Embrace your fellow person and don't be afraid to resemble them. Don't think that you're special, or than anybody else is. We are all animals, and we all want to have good lives.

Remember to be humble. People appreciate people who know how challenging life is, and so showing that you don't suffer from your self-image will show that you know how to live. No one knows everything, and no one has to. All you need to be is the best you that you can be, and to listen well.

Printed in Great Britain
by Amazon